A Day in the Life of Roger Angell

Also by Roger Angell

The Stone Arbor

A Day in the Life of Roger Angell

ROGER ANGELL

New York | THE VIKING PRESS

Contents

A Day in the Life of Roger Angell

A Day in the Life of
Roger Angell

(Mr. Jim Bishop, Author of *The Day Lincoln Was
Shot, A Day in the Life of President Johnson*, etc.,
Grapples Unflinchingly with Still Another Biographee)

6:47 A.M.: The sun, a molten gaseous ball measuring 864,000
miles in diameter, is already up and doing business at its old
stand. In Copenhagen, 92,900,000 miles away from the sun and
3,958 miles east of New York's fashionable upper East Side, the
sunlight falls straight down like a dropped cymbal, clanging
noiselessly off a sidewalk-café table where Jens Nielsen, a fifty-
two-year-old bicycle-clip manufacturer, is tucking a snowy
napkin into his vest. Mr. Nielsen, obeying certain familiar
gastric signals, leans forward and gnashes down pleasurably
on his first bite of *smørrebrød*: lunch has begun. At Weather
Ship Charlie, Lon. 35°30′ west, Lat. 52°45′ north, in the North
Atlantic, the sun at midmorning glowers through a high skin of
clouds, casting a swaying gray lozenge of light onto the bunk
of Seaman Apprentice Orbert Grummond, who is writing a
letter to his mother in East Pharaoh, Kansas. "Dear Mom,"
Grummond writes after several minutes' cogitation. "No news.
This morning we had cirro-stratus at 20,000 feet and chipped
beef for breakfast. Yesterday it looked like rain again, but . . ."
At this moment, the same sun peeps like a débutante over the
ramparts of the abandoned Ruppert Brewery on Manhattan's
Third Avenue. Polite morning shadows tiptoe through the quiet

3

streets of the East Nineties, but here, too, there are stirrings, unmistakable signs of significance. A bus clears its throat somewhere to the north. A pigeon, patrolling a narrow third-floor ledge of an old but tasteful brownstone, pauses in its vigil and cocks an amber optic at a half-shaded window. Within the window, in the South-Facing Bedroom of the Walkup, Roger Angell lies face down on the great Sloane's Bed. One massive arm is flung above his head, the hand open in a curiously boyish gesture of ennui. The stern, lightly lipped mouth lies half open. Roger Angell, quite unconscious of Jens Nielsen's lunch and Seaman Grummond's letter, is asleep. Not for him yet is the business of this day, the awful awareness of details, the knowledge that it is *now*. He is lucky.

Others are asleep here too—Mrs. Angell beside her spouse, a daughter in the adjoining Narrow Room—but already the urgent machinery of living has caught up some in the household. The gray, sagacious elder member of the sleeper's personal guard, known by the code name "Daisy," has heard the pigeon's inquiring *"Croo?"* Instantly awake, she lifts her head from its resting place on the bedroom rug. The slitted yellow eyes come open. The pigeon flaps off, and now there is a stirring and irritable sigh from the right-hand side of the bed. The junior guard, code name "Emma," pads in through the half-open bedroom door, eager for assignment, but a warning glance from her superior stops her in her tracks. The Master, a man of Renaissance moods, does not always react favorably to being awakened by a cold nose stuck in his ear. Now there is a magisterial groan from the bed, and the cats leave the bedroom together, walking fast. In both their minds is the knowledge that the Master, when taken by an early-morning mood of scientific inquiry, sometimes indulges his hobby of high-altitude cat-throwing, stubbornly testing his theory that a feline, when lobbed skyward with the proper degree of spin, will not *always* come down on the bed on all fours. At times, while whirling dizzily near the water-stained ceilings of one of the East Side's most extemporary bedrooms, the senior cat has had to remind herself sharply that none of the Master's behavior is intentionally unbearable. She remembers that this is the same man who, on the evening of January 5th, 1964, impulsively slipped her, at her post under the table, a fragrant sliver of roast chicken taken from his own plate. The fact that he claimed no public credit for this gesture, never permitting mention of it to the press, is as typical of the man as is the fact that it was never repeated. Roger Angell has many attributes of "the boss." Generous, large-footed, and joky, he is still no do-gooder or sap. Cats and people in his administration shape up or get out.

Now the South-Facing Bedroom lies silent again, gathering itself for the day to come. Beside the bed, within reach of Roger Angell's hand, lies a telephone instrument, its dial pierced by a circlet of ten finger holes. By picking up the receiver and swiftly rotating the dial with an intelligent forefinger, the man in the Walkup can instantly provide himself with the voices and the immense burden of information necessary to the business of his day—a plumber's answering service, a delicatessen, the correct time. Across the room, on top of a scarred applewood bureau believed by some historians to have seen combat service in the Salvation Army, there lies eighty-seven cents in change, two paper clips, a hairbrush, an American-made rubberoid comb with three teeth missing, and this day's schedule, decisively scrawled the previous evening by Angell himself on the back of an old bank withdrawal slip. The schedule reads: "Gin. Pay Con Ed. Missing pants at cleaner's?" At first glance, it does not look like a busy day, but there is room in it for innumerable new challenges and chapters. Some of the challenges are simmering at this moment within the enormously wrinkled brain still resting on the right-hand pillow. Fifty blocks south of the Walkup and twenty floors up, in the west ventricle of Megalopolis, lies the office of Roger Angell, editor. It and the surrounding offices are empty now, but in a few hours they will be filled by some of the most unforgiving mentalities in America. On the Rectangular Desk rests a matter for decision—a superfluous and possibly dangerous semicolon in a manuscript. This still ticking crisis would understandably tax any human brain, but yesterday Angell studied the problem unwaveringly, chin on fist, before deciding to sleep on it. Now the twisted seedling of the semicolon lies inside the rich loam bed on the pillow, and today, perhaps, the solution will flower.

8:13 A.M.: Roger Angell sits at the Breakfast Table in one of the East Nineties' most eclectic living-dining rooms. The man has already been up for thirty-six minutes. Moving with typical dispatch, he has brushed thirty-two teeth and, with swift, unerring strokes, removed over seven thousand fragments of whisker from chin and jowls. Now it is the time of the eggs. He looks at the eggs, which have been boiled for exactly two hundred and forty seconds, eye to eye. Evidently satisfied, he transfers his attention to the others at the table. The daughter sits to his left, the wife opposite. There is scarcely a face at this table that is not pleasing to him. By example, long silences, and occasional reprisals, he has welded these women into a family. He knows the capacities of his team. Within minutes, the daughter will rise, make her silent adieux, and depart, behind gigantic circular sunglasses, to keep her sullen diurnal appointment with a Smith-Corona upright, deep in the urban pampas. She leaves behind her, in the Narrow Room, a sweetly feminine and American compost. On the bureau, an empty bottle of L'Interdit lies on its side, halfway between an ashtray containing fourteen cigarette stubs and a small straw basket full of hair rollers, unmatched earrings, and buttons bearing arcane contemporary messages of love and defiance. The bedside table is a scene of girlish disarray, reflecting an eager, scholarly mind—*TV Guide, The Olympia Reader*, a dead moth, and an 8-mm.-film camera containing an undeveloped but arresting closeup of Allen Ginsberg's left ear. The lady of this room is nineteen, an almost-fledged arrow uneasily at rest within the family quiver.

Absent from the Breakfast Table but warmly present in the bulging filing cabinets of Roger Angell's mind is the other daughter, the younger one, who is at this moment spooning prunes into the two-year-old mouth of a boy currently in her charge at one of Cape Cod's most ineluctable "beach" colonies. At sixteen, she is already a passable bedmaker, a barefoot summer soldier in the ranks of the employed. Now she retrieves a fallen prune from the floor and absently reinserts it in the trusting mouth. The tanned shoulder blades rise and fall in a brief sigh. Even if her father were President of the United States, she would still be here spooning prunes, for the homeliest familial task, when tersely limned, speeds narrative and royalties.

At the table, Roger Angell has thrown himself full tilt into *The New York Times.* Names, issues, torrents of data fly up from the gray columns as the dim, four-eyed gaze, flicking from left to right, absorbs, considers, forgets. At the far end of the table, the lady of the house sips coffee. She is a pretty woman who eats pretty. Soon she too will take her leave, coifed and A-shaped, to meet her economic responsibilities, for everyone in the Angell boat pulls full weight. Within her Gucci pocketbook, the Bonwit's charge plate confidently awaits its noontime airing.

Now the newspaper at the head of the table is lowered briefly, and Angell clears his throat. A thought is on the way to his tongue. The mouth opens. "The Giants," it says, "is dead." Even before the words are out, Angell's quick-striding consciousness has flicked to the next column, where it absorbs more technical intelligence—news of a tennis tournament. Into the Sportsman's mind there floats a clear image of a memorable double fault served by him the previous Saturday, at set point, on a green *en-tout-cas* court eighty-five miles to the north-northeast. The well-netted balls hang in his mind like gasping shad. He rubs his towering forehead and sighs, remembering the aces that once flew off the racquet of a promising editor-athlete named Roger Angell.

The pages of the *Times* rustle and turn. There is a pause at the fashion page, and abruptly the stern face breaks into a creased smile, like a Mark Cross overnight bag being opened.

In a soft, pumalike tone, Angell murmurs, "I think Twiggy is a stick." The front door slams; the daughter has gone. The two cats leave the room together, padding on burglar-quick paws. Mrs. Angell is in the kitchen, clashing dishes. The man at the head of the table looks up, puzzled. Breakfast, it seems, is over.

9:07 A.M.: The first Gristede delivery bikes rattle up Madison Avenue on their life-giving rounds. In Copenhagen, Jens Nielsen nervously paces the worn carpeting of his dusty office. On Weather Ship Charlie, Seaman Grummond stares irritably off at the horizon and bites his nails. Both are waiting to resume their parts in this drama of the present. Is it possible that they have been forgotten? Roger Angell is alone in the Walkup. Wearing pale-fawn boxer shorts, he stands in front of the kaleidoscopically jumbled tie rack inside the closet door of the South-Facing Bedroom. Low-key reps, rich silks, brightly checked ginghams come before his gaze. This is the time of the tie, and Angell the Dandy does not hurry. There is reputation to be sustained in this area, for Roger Angell knows that a junior reporter, hopelessly overmatched in a struggle for office hard-worsted supremacy, was once heard to mutter petulantly, "No one has *ever* seen the tops of Angell's socks." Today, however, the lightning of decision does not strike. Yawning, Angell shuffles to the bureau and begins to pull on a clean shirt. One arm is in the shirt when his eye falls on the scribbled day's calendar. Now the lean-shanked frame swings into action. He picks up the telephone and dials the dry cleaner's. The voice on the other end recognizes the caller and replies at once, ready for action. Inefficiency is raw skin at the Walkup.

Like many middle-aged literary men, Angell is unafraid to descend to the use of plain language in time of stress. "Hey," he rasps, the voice rising dangerously, "where the hell are my gray pants?"

Accustomed to brusque demands from this quarter, the voice on the phone suggests a possible solution. The tall instigator of the inquiry demurs flatly. The voice placates, rephrases, suggests. Angell, the half-on, half-off shirt flying behind him, strides to his wife's closet and finds there, swathed in Pliofilm and hidden between two freshly pressed dresses, the erroneously placed garment. He returns to the phone. No social amenities are brooked at such a time. "Right," he snaps, and hangs up.

Roger Angell has been awake for an hour and forty minutes, and one-third of the day's calendar has already become history. Now a weariness, a mood of introspection typical of sensitive men, comes over him. It seems to him that the knuckle of the day has already been gnawed. He spots the gawky, half-dressed figure in the bedroom mirror, and looks away. Unaccountably, the sleeved arm comes out of the shirt. The shirt is thrown aside. Angell sits on the bed and studies his Gothic feet. The man on the bed considers the issues that lie in wait for him. He thinks of the semicolon still dangerously coiled on the snake pit of the Rectangular Desk. He remembers the unresolved riddle of the necktie. Once, the man in the Walkup would have charged pell-mell at these problems, but slowly, steadily, he has come to accept the truth that everything cannot, or at least need not, be accomplished at once.

The wise gray guard slips noiselessly into the room and takes up her post on the rug. She watches while the Master lies back on the tastefully flowered bedspread. Then, with an infinitely delicate gesture of contempt, she lowers her head onto her paws. Across the room, the great feet are swung up onto the bed and comfortably crossed. Now there is a sigh. Now a soft snore rises into the morning air. Roger Angell's day—or certainly more than enough of it—is over.

Your Horoscope

(More Unsolicited Guidance from Out There)

Taurus (Apr. 21-May 21)

With Venus ascendant and frozen pork-belly futures holding firm, this is a week for modest household chores. Unkink and clean all shoelaces, not overlooking the lacing on your football. Recaulk the dog's water dish, the tank on the Water Pik, etc. Toward the end of the week, chair casters may be inspected in relative safety. Because of an enigmatic (or quietly amused) aspect of Mercury, it would be wiser not to get dressed before nightfall.

Gemini (May 22-June 21)

Sorry, Gemini people, but still no advice for you. Eleven weeks now and still not a word from the Stars for this dormant house! Oh, well, things are bound to start popping soon. Meantime, try not to do anything at all.

Cancer (June 22-July 22)

A confused period for you normally ebullient Crabs. Purely social occupations will help keep your mind off insomnia, erasers, and eastbound watercraft. Damp bathing suits may prove annoying on Tuesday, but try to keep your composure at all costs. Some rumpling of the eyebrows may be observed upon arising. An elderly terrier will be thinking about you over the weekend.

Leo (July 23-Aug. 23)

Your best week of the entire year for sheer recklessness. Obey that wiggy impulse! Vault subway turnstiles, dress up in your wife's clothes, tell off a policeman, coat yourself in peanut butter—it doesn't matter, for the Stars say this is your time to howl! A meditative period will descend late in the week, when you may wish to consult legal and medical experts.

Virgo (Aug. 24-Sept. 23)

Those not born under this sign would do well to visit all their Virgo friends before 4:20 P.M. on Monday, but to stay well away thereafter. As for you Virgos—well, astrology is still a difficult science, and maybe we're reading these signs wrong, ha, ha! Good luck to you all.

Libra (Sept. 24-Oct. 23)

A time for inwardness and mental housecleaning. Try to rid your mind of excess baggage. Forget about the Diet of Worms. Forget factoring, the cambium layer, Deanna Durbin, and Sibyl Colefax. Get rid of the Rock of Chickamauga, the color of Ventnor Avenue, and the words of "Bibbidi-Bobbidi-Boo." Throw out Gantner Wikies, Engine Charlie Wilson, and "anent." Try never to think about tundra. What a lot of trash you've been carrying around in the old bean! No wonder you can't make any money.

Scorpio (Oct. 24-Nov. 22)

Mars will be entering this house shortly after lunch on Tuesday, so you Scorpios, already habitually suspicious, would do well to double your guard in this period. If your friends have been whispering about you in the past, just think what they're saying now! Laundrymen and Celts may try to bilk you, possibly through the mails. An agent of a Balkan power, perhaps posing as a close relative, will try to blow nerve gas through your telephone receiver while you sleep. Next week will be worse.

Sagittarius (Nov. 23-Dec. 21)

All you Archers—so good-looking, so impetuous, so lovably harum-scarum—have been making a perfect hash of your lives ever since the moon slipped off your cusp way back in March, 1964. Time to come down to earth! This week, try to study some modest, everyday object and appreciate its true nature. Study one of your thumbs, for instance. Not the handsomest of all your fingers, perhaps, but one that does its job, day in and day out, without fanfare or vaingloriousness. See how wrinkled it has grown around the knuckle, but with never a word of complaint. You are lucky to have stubby Mr. Thumbkin (a typical Gemini) working for you, and you might do well to emulate his patience. If you were a dog or a fox, your thumb would be way up by your wrist somewhere, and absolutely useless. What a lesson for us all!

Capricorn (Dec. 22-Jan. 20)

Pablo Casals, Senator Mondale, Renata Tebaldi, Willie McCovey, Howard Hughes, Ava Gardner, President Nasser, and President Nixon were all born under this sign, which rules the knees. The best guide to your week is to watch these fellow-Capricorns closely, for if things go well for them, they will go well for you, too. If they all have a terrible week—broken cello strings, blocked legislation, tonsillitis, popups, etc.—so will you, in your own tiny way. You may find it difficult to discover much in common with each and every one of these Goat people, but that's the way astrology works, so stop complaining.

Aquarius (Jan. 21-Feb. 19)

Persons born under Aquarius are restless, indolent, fond of water sports, pleasing, and agreeable. Their greatest fault is procrastination. This will be a fine week for you to mooch around the house quietly, smoothing over family arguments and making friends with the milkman. Take a nap or look out the window for a while. Maybe you could get in a little surfing. On the other hand, why don't you wait and go surfing *next* week? What the hell.

Pisces (Feb. 20-Mar. 20)

This week climaxes a series of highly favorable indications for fish and Fish people. Go to the aquarium, take up fly-tying, buy a pair of guppies. Try codfish balls for breakfast—delicious! On Friday, before the onset of your coming counter-period of drought, why not throw a mammoth "Fish Fry"? Invite Hamilton Fish, Bob Trout, Ben Pollack, Dick Bass, Jean Shrimpton, Aldo Ray, Hulan Jack, Congressman Pike, etc. How they will laugh when they all "get it"!

Aries (Mar. 21-Apr. 20)

The Stars tell us that during the coming six to eight weeks the Indonesian government will be overthrown by a Mormon clique; two European chiefs of state will be unmasked as C.I.A. agents; Liverpool will be ravaged by locusts; Akron, Ohio, will slide into the Atlantic Ocean (you can't argue with the Stars); the International Monetary Fund will be rocked by a Profumo-type scandal; and an oil slick will imperil the Wollman Memorial Rink. In view of the world-shaking nature of these impending events, how can you pushy, invariably selfish Rams keep asking astrologists for help with your petty personal affairs? Enough, already! Can't you see we're busy?

Ivy

(Evidences of a Severe Literary Syndrome Experienced after Absorbing, in One Delicious Gulp, the Four Alexandrian Novels, *Justine, Balthazar, Mountolive,* and *Clea,* by Mr. Lawrence Durrell, to Whom Is Offered a Deep Levantine Bow)

Landscape-Tones: thumbsmudged grays athwart the walls of the unswept corridor; fuchsine pink of the floorward-pointing arrow above the door of the awaited, chain-rattling elevator. Mudspatter tans and greens on the okapi flank of the evening taxi. Remembered lilac mauves in the flecks of her eyes as she lay, softly sighing over some imagined slight, in her charming accustomed attitude of exhaustion. Bruise-purples on the shoulders of the wheeling pigeons, short scimitars slicing the white sky of this too-Western littoral.

Copernicus, the milkman, has been missing for a week. His last delivery consisted of two pints of strawberry yoghurt, a gnostic warning of his disaffection. Another mystagogue gone from the Cabal.

Cat-dust afloat between the ramparts of the timeless, senectuous tenements, caught and made golden by a random sunshaft, and below, in the dry jungle of smashed hedges and stillborn philodendron, ravaged by the sneakered *fellaheen* of the quarter, the animals themselves, self-consumed by the yellow hunger of their ancient eyes. She used to watch them from our back window, my sweet voyeuse, her entire body quivering in sympathy for their loneliness, and I would sense myself abandoned again. Ivy, the Nefertiti-eared. How can I face her now?

Crumbie, the subway motorman, sensed the truth, or the lie, in our relationship. Once, asprawl in my sling chair, his vast belly comfortably between his knees, and his humorous, rheumy, jongleur's eyes alight with the inner wisdom, the thesaurian omniscience that all my acquaintances seem to possess, he waved one of his great cuffed gloves at her as she lay asleep beside me, her head on my lap. "You think she loves you, don't you, *mon vieux?*" he said, his voice rumbling out of the caverns of his chest like an onrushing E train. "Love is your obsession. Your old noddle whirls with it day and night, the needle scratching out the same meretricious *javas*. My poor littérateur, you confuse possession with passion, convenience with adoration. Mark my words, Aeneas, you will do your innocent Dido a great hurt one day." Titubating slightly in his chair, he reached down between his feet for his glass, which was characteristically empty (he had a great thirst for the native elixirs), and held it out toward me. "You got any more *phabst*, buddy?" he said, smiling wickedly.

He was right, of course. I knew it, though I denied it thumpingly; even at the height of my shrill recusance, I could hear a piquant, subterranean *scritch-scritch!* within me—the rat-gnawings of suspicion and betrayal. How could I doubt the love of one who lay so innocently beside me now, one who had often rewarded me with a trusting, housewifely snore as I read aloud to her from my annotated volumes of de Sade and Rider Haggard? But for every trust there is a countering suspicion within us, love's antimatter. I remembered mysteries, evasions. From whom did she obtain such a gift as that uncut, sanguineous, Persian-red *bifteck* I saw her carrying, wordlessly ecstatic, across the croquet lawn of the Summer Embassy in Katonah early one Sunday morning? I never dared ask her. I have even suspected that she and Cloya might love each other. A bat thought, brushing my face in the dark. Once I surprised Cloya proffering her a Necco wafer, and sometimes on winter evenings I have intercepted a look between them, a feminine arrow of understanding and commiserating sympathy. Ouf! What confusions, what ferberian profundities!

Crumbie was still watching me. Could he know what evil
surprise I had planned for Ivy? Guiltily, I looked down at her
seamed, dew-lapped muzzle, the beloved profile of *ma jolie laide,*
and then I awakened her and she and I played gaily
before him, as if to exorcise, with her rubber bone, the witch
truth that we all recognized. I remember that as we romped
together, two acolytes of love hurrying through the enforced
rituals of our order under the wise eye of an aged archimandrite,
Crumbie murmured, "How typical of you to own a bulldog.
Especially a bitch. Outrage is your forte, as are antipodes. Thus
your effeminate battler, your womanish Hercules. Of course, she
is far too good for you."

Even as he spoke, there fell a sudden bumbling of thunder
from the flat, sullen sky without—an ominous throat-clearing
of the gods preceding the passing of some awful sentence. And
now the deed is done, the sentence executed, and I must go
this afternoon to Dr. Balsamic's establishment and face Ivy,
she who understood almost nothing (no more than the impatient
reader of some significant palimpsest) of what the hell was going
on between us.

Season of the stocking-ladder. Winter-clank in the starved
steampipes. Faint effluvium of mixed vetiver and pot from the
empty marzipan jar. Rain squalls in the West Fifties, dappling
the roofs of the versicolorate sports cars clustered like rank,
overripe fruit in their dusty orchards. Cloya's face seen upside-
down in her full Martini glass, an avid water-lily.

Pierrepont, the gharry driver, is dead, possibly by his own
hand. He was found slumped over the wheel of his cab, the
coils of his *narguileh* twisted tightly about his aristocratic, Hittite
neck. He had been a great womanizer, but he had been forced
to deny his appetites cruelly. He confessed to me once that
he suffered agonies from couvade and that his analyst (his
"psyche-twist," as he called him) had warned him that he might
not survive another confinement. Sad.

Aleicester, the poet, has at last finished the mighty palindrome that has entirely engaged his attention for the past eight years. Cloya brought it to me at dawn last Tuesday and I read it through in six hours, all the way from its brave, Homeric opening statement "T. Eliot, top bard, notes putrid tang," to the great dying fall of its final line, ". . . Gnat-dirt upset on drab pot toilet." Cloya tells me it will probably never be published; Aleicester, half mad with his vision, has already wrangled with his publisher, claiming that since the work can be read backward as well as forward he must receive double royalties. Ironic end to one so talented, so bored.

Did I say "too-Western littoral" earlier? Odd! Just this morning I received another communication from Pinchbeck, the novelist, in which he urges me to move eastward. Near the end of this typically assertive document—a high-heaped interlinear correcting certain literate but misconceived comments I had scrawled in the margins of a fugitive work by Rhodmek Kün, the old bard of this narrow, fluminose island—he writes: "Novelists, like horticulturists, must find the proper climate for their little crop of hybrid conceits. If you persist in planting your lush tropical blooms by the sidewalks of a Hyperborean stone city, you will not be entitled to the luxury of surprise or hurt when preoccupied residents turn coldly away from your finest blossoms muttering, 'They don't even look real.' Your own verb-garden, your overmulched nouns, require a feverish Levantine sun, the swollen profligacies of some Eastern delta. Plant your flowers there—in Smyrna, Aleppo, or Alexandria— let them burgeon in all their premeditated brilliance, and *then* watch the tourists trample your borders! See them sniff, note the shocked delight in their eyes as they ogle each purple stalk, each velvet petal, each naughty stamen, and listen to them as they exclaim, 'How lovely, how wicked, how *true!*' "

Pinchbeck is listenable, of course, but I must confess that I suspect him of jealousy. For one thing, he writes so much like me—implacably Gongoresque, logorrheac to a fault. And then, Copernicus has told me that Pinchbeck once indulged in a bitter public outburst against my concept of the novel as

a five-sided continuum—the quincunx book, with four char-
acters (or four volumes) spinning in orbit about the fixed
center dot of events, like a die flung down on the green baize
table of truth.

I must leave now; she will be waiting. The skin over my
temples feels tautly stretched—a certain warning of the onset
of *cafard*. It takes me forever to get going these days; one might
even suspect me of wishing to inflate the meaning of each
action, however trivial or fascinating, through cunctation and
quiddity.

Out, then, again into the streets. I turn westward, toward
the sun, stumping bravely toward Dr. Balsamic's antiseptic
couloirs. Mica-sheen from the minarets of the Squibb Building.
Below the conflagration of afternoon sky, below the great Wee-
hawken Corniche, the seared, exhausted traffic-swarm, thrilling
the belly with the blare of its impatient horns. Squadrons, platoons, entire divisions of pedestrians, package-bearing, news-
papered, come clicking toward me, and I notice again how
blurred, how impalpable they all seem in the ambient mistral
that blows across this city at all seasons from the slopes of Mt.
Simile. On the corner, Gepetto, the bearded convert, winks
to me as he hurries past on his way to evensong—the Copt on
the beat.

I come at last to the address, pass under the chaste, fly-specked
sign ARISTOTLE BALSAMIC, D.V.M., and step into the white-walled
foyer and the clean, masochistic scent of iodoform. The Dravidian
receptionist ushers me into Balsamic's empty consulting room,
where I sit briefly, listening to the yelps and bayings of hell
that fall faintly here upon my abashed ears. Palpitant, I hear
a step and a shuffle without, and they enter, Balsamic resembling
a sleepy-eyed snowy owl in his sterile gown, and Ivy almost
hidden behind him, her head low.

No bandage. I had expected bandages. My waif is thinner,
etiolated by her experience, but when she sees me her gazelle eyes
light up bravely. But she does not throw herself into my arms

in her customary abandoned *abrazo*. It is as I had known it would be: forgiveness was too much to expect.

I must speak. "How is she, Doctor?"

"Fine," Balsamic says. "No complications. You can take her home now."

"But then what?" I cry out. "What will she think of me for putting her through all this? I mean, what about the *spirit*, the inner maelstrom? Isn't there danger of post-operative synecdoche?"

Balsamic regards me skeptically, looking like—well, like a skeptical doctor. "Listen," he says wearily, "it was perfectly routine. It's normal to spay a dog of her age. I recommended it, and I'm sure I was right."

I take the leash from him and make one more effort. "Doesn't it mean *anything* to her?"

"Not a blessed thing. Oh, if she seems to have any trouble sleeping tonight, you might slip her a Bufferin, but that's all. In a few days she'll have forgotten all about this." He must perceive some vestigial shimmer—could it be disappointment?—in my eyes, for he steps forward and places a friendly, scrubbed, Philistine hand on my arm. "Look, fella," he says in his emollient baritone, "you writers, particularly you vocabulary-enrichers, ought to go easy on yourselves. All this high-class suffering and speculating, I mean. You're so damned sure that everybody is chock-full of passion and guilt and memory and all like that, when most of the time—almost all the time, if you ask me—they're not thinking of anything but their next can of Ken-L-Ration. Keep that in mind—O.K.?"

I nod, and Ivy and I take our leave. Outside, darkness has veiled the aged face of the courtesan streets, and the buildings above us cast down an autumnal pollen of yellow lights. The leash slack between us, we turn automatically and prophetically toward the East, each wincing faintly from our interior wounds. We are both exhausted, and no wonder.

AFTERWORD TO *"Ivy"*

Lawrence Durrell may be surprised to learn that he is not the only British author to have been slighted in this slipshod forgery. The visionary palindromist introduced above as "Aleicester, the poet" is modeled not on one of Mr. Durrell's maimed romantics but on Mr. Alastair Reid, the distinguished Scottish poet and author, who wrote the two-way lines quoted here. His "mighty palindrome," while actually requiring something less than six hours to read, deserves to be quoted in full, for it is the most stimulating long-distance shuttle in our language: "T. Eliot, top bard, notes putrid tang emanating, is sad. I'd assign it a name: 'Gnat-dirt upset on drab pot toilet.'"

Exemplary readers who persist to the final chapter of this book will find Mr. Reid still smiling graciously and anonymously as he is again victimized in exactly the same way. Few authors have displayed equal courage when confronted with such a reckless kleptomania.

The Floto Letters

Dear Mayor Floto:

Starting this new "Vox Pop" letters column in the newspaper so citizens can write to you direct about the conditions of their city is nothing but another cheap "politician's trick," but just the same I think I will send you my "beef." Nothing runs anymore in this town, and that goes especially for the Scarlatti Fountain out on West Inglenook (near where I live), which is a disgrace. The pools are all dried and cracked and full of trash, the water pipes and nozzles are rusted away, and somebody has broke off the composer's nose and part of the harp that belonged to the Muse. Another nice old part of the city ruined and another insult to the Italian people. What are you going to do about it?

Burned Up

Dear Burned:

As you may know, the problem you mention has already been dealt with. The party or parties unknown who stole the Scarlatti Fountain last Thursday night are still at large, but Police Chief Hackbart assures me that his department has several promising leads and that the miscreants will soon be brought to justice. In the meantime, decent citizens like yourself can find some comfort in the knowledge that there is a very poor current market for late-nineteenth-century rococo sculpture, and, likewise, that the cost and trouble of repairing, installing, and furtively operating a fifty-eight-foot vertical-spray fountain will detract considerably from any private aesthetic comfort these despoilers may have envisaged. I believe that this entire episode constitutes a lesson for us all, illustrating the value of patience in solving urban problems. Frankly, the question of what to do about the decaying Scarlatti Fountain had been allowed to hang fire for some time, ever since a deadlocked hearing of the Municipal Arts Board in 1927. Up to last week, the matter still seemed hopeless, yet today it has been entirely cleared up—cleared up, I may point out, at no cost to the taxpayers. As Scarlatti himself might have said, *Allegro non troppo*!

John J. Floto

Dear Mayor Floto:

I have been raising tropical fish for twenty years (it's my hobby), but ever since you got into City Hall my danios have been dying off. Now, just lately, the guppies are going too.

Fishwife

Dear Mrs. Fishwife:

Dr. Krementz, Assistant Freshwater Curator at the Northside Aquarium, tells me that twenty is very old for a guppy, so I do not think you should feel too much sadness or guilt about the passing of your little friends. Probably it's "all for the best," as the saying goes. As for the other possible interpretation of your brief but stimulating letter, Krementz thinks it unlikely that domestic piscine longevity is much affected by municipal politics. He adds, however, there is very little empirical data on this question. How did you vote in the last election?

J. J. F.

Hey Mr. Mayor-Man:

What's happening, baby? I guess you know this town is on a bum trip—narcs everywhere and no good weed going unpunished. Bad, *bad* scenes, man! The Acapulco up to $45 and none in sight. No Great Seedless Purple. No Tampico Taupe, no Valparaiso Violet, no Yggdrasill Yellow. Your best bread only gets a bag of stalks and pocket lint, with so many seeds you like to set your pants on fire. You trying to drive us onto the speedway, Poppa? I mean, how is a good quiet head going to get his head together?

Smokey the Bear

Dear Smokey:

Even though my opponent for this office swore that grass would grow on the streets if I were elected, possession is still a stiff rap in this state and I have to "groove" on the law. I hope you saw a recent news photograph of me in the act of destroying some two million dollars' worth of illegal marijuana, which our local agents had intercepted in a shipment of frozen instant enchiladas. On that occasion, in an impromptu address to several reporters, cameramen, and police officers gathered at the Municipal Incinerator to witness the confiscation, I stated my firm belief that each of us should be capable of attaining a state of high spirits *without recourse to artificial and illegal stimulants or narcotics.* Then, after I had lighted the blaze, our group ascended to the roof of the Incinerator Building, where I wished to inspect a defective chimney that has been giving us some trouble of late; I'm sure you know my position on clean air. More photographs were taken there while I discussed repair of the chimney (it was indeed in bad shape, emitting a heavy pall of smoke from several fissures) with our Environmental Control people. Someone then remarked on the fine view of the River and the Eutawpa Hills one is offered from the roof of the Incinerator Building, and we all concurred enthusiastically. The Deputy Incineration Engineer even stated that he had never even been *aware* of the view until that instant, which caused a hearty laugh. In the end, most of us stayed up on the roof for the rest of the afternoon and well into the evening (despite fits of coughing attributable to the faulty chimney) while we indulged in thoughtful conversations about the beauty of our old town, the nearness of the stars, the distinctly reptilian appearance of Lower Marpless Drive, etc. This pleasant interlude, in fact, caused me to be more than two hours late for the Annual Corn Planters' Ball!

I cite this incident because I think it suggests a sound policy for us all. My little homily about man's capacity for natural, self-induced euphoria seemed to strike a common chord, encouraging each of us—reporters, police officers, civic servants—

to pause there on the roof and appreciate for once the simple
daily wonders that surround us. I tell you, Smokey, it was *great*
up there. Wow, what a view. Wow, wow!

J. J. F.

Dear Mayor Floto:

Everywhere, the erosion of comfort—nay, of mere convenience
—deepens. We live up on Delancey Plains, supposedly a "good
address." Lately, however, there has been a shocking decline
in services, which seems to be all too typical of conditions all
over our city. First the doormen vanished. Then cabs ceased
to appear. Then our phone went on the fritz. Last week, no
hot water. Now there's something wrong with the lights. Where
are those everyday amenities that used to make city life so
pleasant? What is a civilized man to do nowadays?

Old Settler

Dear Mr. Settler:

One thing a civilized man might do is go to the window
and take a careful look outside, noting especially if there are
any new "empty places" in the neighborhood. The entire
Delancey Plains area was condemned eleven months ago, to
make room for the new Frobisher International Airport, and
demolition of the last buildings is scheduled to begin next
Monday morning.

Let's all try a little harder to keep on our toes—O.K.?

J. J. F.

Dear Mayor Floto:

The city garbage truck that collects on our block has no
American Flag on it. Our police and firemen are not afraid
to show where their hearts belong, but some of these sanitation
types are too stuck on themselves even to put up a little
decal of Old Glory on their windshields. Maybe they'd rather
make their rounds in Hanoi!

Mrs. Delight Jorgensen

Dear Mrs. Jorgensen:

Good for you! It's high time you real patriots rared up on your hind legs and showed us what you're made of. I'm sure that a person of your type will be pleased to know that your letter brought some fast results. The Character Committee of the Sanitation Workers Union launched a full investigation of the incident, and the three-man crew that used to serve your street has already been subjected to disciplinary action. Faced with undeniable evidence of flaglessness, two of these sanitation men made a full apology and confession of error; they have been permitted to remain in the Department, on a probationary basis, as apprentice manhole-flangers. The third member of the crew, however, proved to be intransigent. A thin young man with a droopy mustache, he appeared before the committee wearing tie-dyed jeans and love beads, and announced that he was joining a commune in Oregon, where he would devote himself henceforward to "cleaning out his own attic." Before turning in his badge, he played a short selection on a nose flute and then recited this piece of verse:

> ". . . in pool and rut peel parches
> Squandering ooze to squeezed dough,
>   crust, dust; stanches, starches
> Squadroned masks and manmarks
>   treadmire toil there
> Footfretted in it. Million-fuelèd,
>   nature's bonfire burns on."

The Character Committee ruled that this confusing and anarchic view of the sanitation man's profession (I am told it is a fragment of a poem by G. M. Hopkins) be stricken from the record of the hearing; it then voted its heartfelt thanks to you, Mrs. Jorgensen, for "ridding the Department of one real weirdo."

J. J. F.

Dear Mayor Floto:

I just gave up on this city. This morning the alarm went off, but instead of getting up I lay in bed awhile. I thought about getting dressed, getting my coffee, getting to the bus, riding the bus, getting off the bus and changing to the subway, going up to the office. Thought about how it looks outside these days while everybody's waiting for the bus, with the lumpy old wornout snow still there and all that's piled up on it since way back last month, and more black gock falling on it out of the sky while you're standing there, and how the air smells dead all the time now. Thought about maybe no newspaper to read because somebody's always on strike again and won't deliver the papers. Thought about shoving into the bus (and maybe the bus being late again) and me afraid I don't have the 89 cents exact fare ready and scared the bus driver will yell at me and throw me off the bus if I don't. Thought about old commuting gents in baggy coats and rubbers looking tired on the bus, and did I have a token (another 89 cents) for the subway, and then the push out of the bus and down the steps, and the cold air and dirty papers blowing up out of the subway. Then waiting down in the subway (and maybe the train being late again), and being jammed in the car with all those faces looking at you, and maybe somebody in there shouting out loud to themselves or laughing or maybe *saying* something to you because there are so many crazies around now. Thought about the train stopping in the dark tunnel and maybe getting stuck there for a while, nobody knows how long, and the crowded car all full of breathing. Then (still lying in bed) I thought, Why try? Why go to work? What's better there than here? So I stayed in bed (still here) and wrote you this letter. What's happened to our city, Mayor Floto? How did things get this way? What's going to happen to me now, for the love of God?

Patrick Mulvany

Dear Mr. Mulvany:

This has been a tough week, and your letter hasn't helped at all. This is just to tell you that I am getting tired of trouble-makers like you. To be frank, I don't think you *have* a job; I think you're an unemployed writer. Do you think I can't recognize periphrasis when I see it? You and your "old commuting gents in baggy coats and rubbers looking tir⸱ ⸱ on the bus"! Who do you think you are—Yeats? Jimmy Breslin?

Listen, Mulvany, I don't know how things got this way, because nobody does. The motto of this administration is something I swiped from a *real* writer, a fellow by the name of John Cage: "The truth is that everything causes everything else. We do not speak therefore of one thing causing another."

As for your last question, it might interest you to know that I read your damned letter out loud to the Board of Aldermen at our meeting this morning. We then drew the yarrow stalks (lately, we've found the "I Ching" more and more helpful in our deliberations), and what came up for you was K'un ("Oppression" or "Exhaustion"), a hexagram that includes a six at the beginning ("One sits oppressed under a bare tree and strays into a gloomy valley . . ."), a nine in the fifth place ("His nose and feet are cut off. Oppression at the hands of the man with the purple knee bands . . ."), and a six at the top ("He is oppressed by creeping vines. He moves uncertainly. . . . If one feels remorse over this and makes a start, good fortune comes"). Need I interpret? If I were you, Mulvany, I'd hop out of bed this instant and beat it out of town.

> *J. J. F.*
> (Purple Knee Bands)

Dear Mayor Floto:

What's happened to our kids? The other night I was watching the Cormorant basketball game on TV, and my son Byram, age 17, came into the room just as I am yelling something at Bingo Moussorgsky, the Cormorants' coach, who had just made another bonehead move to help the team move nearer the old cellar, and Byram laughed. "What are you laughing at?" I asked, explaining that the Cormorants were about to lose their ninth straight. "I don't care," said Byram, "and I am laughing at you." Then we "had words" and my beer got spilled on the davenport.

If our schools and churches would teach some decency and

respect for parents, there wouldn't be all these demonstrations, dropouts, pornography, and trouble on the streets. And if you bleeding hearts in City Hall would spend some money to build just one Champ club for this city, instead of the losers we got now, then maybe kids would stay home with their old man once in a while and watch the game, and we wouldn't have so much immorality and crime. Right?

Big Fred

Dear Fred:

Your letter has opened my eyes. I think you're dead right, and to prove it I have just appointed Bingo Moussorgsky to fill the vacant $80,000 sinecure as our Commissioner of Housing. This may not help our slum clearance program much, but what the hell—*nothing* seems to help the slums these days, eh, Fred? This way, at least, the Cormorants will get a new coach. I think they'll need a good one, because according to information now on my desk the team is about to be subjected to a massive campaign of round-the-clock demonstrations, picketing, boycotts, sit-ins, and harangues by the Women's Liberation Front, which is charging the Cormorants with discrimination in hiring practices. How does that grab you? Don't you think that Byram will be more interested in the Cormorants when they become the first heterosexual team in the N.B.A.? Don't you think that our passionate involvement in all-male professional teams suggests a hysterical-homosexual fantasy buried deep in the American Unconscious? Why are you afraid of cellars? I suggest that you talk over all these difficult questions with your son. Everything is changing these days, Fred, believe you me.

By the way, the Moussorgsky appointment is my final one as Mayor. Your letter and most of the other citizens' letters sent to me over the past six months have finally convinced me that city life, while perhaps still rewarding for some, no longer offers the same enrichment, zest, and challenge to high accomplishment that it once did for me. Or, as Mrs. Floto put it the other day, "Who wants to be Chief Kook in Kooksville?"

By the time you read this, we will already be in residence, along with the children, in a somewhat smaller settlement out in Oregon, where I plan to undertake a regimen of fasting and meditation at the feet of an erstwhile young colleague of mine who also recently retired from the *faubourgs*. Please let me know how the Cormorants make out. Or don't—see if I care.

John J. Floto

Over My Head

My agent, Morrie, came to see me in the clubhouse after a night game in May. I was surprised to see him; he hadn't done any business for me all season. Last year, it was different. After I'd hung up that good E.R.A., third best in the league, and pitched three shutout innings in the All-Star game, I was a hot item, and Morrie kept me busy. I did comedy bits for Vitalis and Supp-hose, made guest shots with Carson and Griffin, appeared on panels to talk about juvenile delinquency and air-pollution and missile deployment, and all that stuff. It was a groove. But this spring I was a holdout for five weeks, and I never did get trained right. I had this sore arm all through April. Then I got bombed out in Oakland and Kansas City on the same swing west, and I lost my spot in the rotation. It got so I'd been picking up the paper every day to see if I'd been traded to Montreal. So why would Morrie want to see me?

"Buzzie bay-bee!" Morrie said. "How's the arm?"

"It fell off last week," I said. "I'm having it embalmed."

"How'd you like to make a wad of cash?" he asked.

"Doing what—selling birdseed door to door?"

"No, Buzz. It's a special deal, something brand-new. There's a couple of thousand clams in it for you. Listen, you ever read that magazine *Sports Illusory*?"

"Are you *kidding*?"

"Let me put it another way," Morrie said. "Did you read that book by the writer who pitched against an all-star big-league team in an exhibition game? That society cat, George Plimpton? You know his thing. Like he hadn't pitched since school, and he wanted to see what it would feel like out there throwing to Willie Mays and all them, and then write about it. He put it all in a book, his first book. It's called *Out of My League*."

"I know about it, but I haven't read it," I said. "It's even in paperback. I've been meaning to get it. Marianne Moore gave it a terrific plug, I think in the *New York Review of Books.*" I was getting interested.

"O.K.," Morrie said. "Now, here's the MacGuffin. *Sports Illusory* wants you to do the same thing, almost. They want you to spend a day working on the staff of a magazine, just like a big-time writer or editor. Then you write a piece about it for them. You dig? It's a hell of a switch, and it backs up their big theme that ballplayers are funky, high-type Joes, interested in the arts and all, just like their average readers. They'll pay two big rocks for the job. How does it hit you?"

"Well. . . ." I said. I tried to sound dubious, but the truth is my heart was racing with excitement. It was crazy and it would take nerve, but what big-leaguer could turn down a chance like this? Like every red-blooded American ballplayer, I've always wanted to be a writer. I've read every word Norman Mailer has written for *Life.* I never miss Gore Vidal or Bill Buckley on the tube. And plenty of ballplayers have made it in the world of letters, haven't they? Look at Jim Bouton. Look at Eugene McCarthy. Way back in my sandlot days, I knew all about Jim Brosnan, the Cincinnati pitcher who wrote those books. I even copied some of his mannerisms—the way he muttered those lines from Pound and Eliot when he glared down at the batters. "What's the magazine I'd be working for?" I managed to ask.

"It's the best, Buzz," he said. "The *Dijon Review.*"

"Wow!" I murmured. This *was* the big league! The *Dijon Review*—the most intellectual, the most shrill, the most insufferable of the little reviews! I could feel the sweat beginning to trickle down my wrists, and I knew I'd lose my nerve if I thought about it a minute longer. "O.K.," I said, looking up at Morrie and trying to manage a smile. "I'll do it."

The day set for my adventure was a Monday in June, an open date on the team's schedule, and the intervening weeks flew by all too fast for my heightened state of nerves. More than once, I picked up the telephone to call Morrie and tell him I had thought better of the whole foolhardy scheme, but some curious sense of pride always made me put it down again. After all, I'd remind myself, I was introspective, well read, full of normal literary ambitions. Even if I got my ears knocked off, it would be something to tell my grandchildren about—the day I matched my taste against the best aesthetes of my time. I found it hard to concentrate on my work; sitting in the bullpen during a Sunday doubleheader, I would lose track of the score. The roar of the crowd and the harsh cries of the peanut venders would fade from my ears, replaced in my mind by the crisp crackle of manuscripts, the sibilant crawl of blue pencils across paper, and the civilized murmur of epigrams and barbed rejoinders. Once, in New York, I slipped out of my room at five in the morning and walked through the dawn-swept streets and found myself at last standing in front of the West Side brownstone that houses the editorial offices of the *Dijon Review*. "In there," I whispered to myself, eying the temple, "just a few days from now. . . ." Inside my pockets, my typing fingers were tapping out unconscious arpeggios.

In the last few days, the realities of plans and training helped to steady me. I went all over town to costume myself correctly—striped bells and fringed Custer tunic from the East Village, granny shades from Meyrowitz, Gucci loafers. I bought a black shirt at a police outfitter's on Spring Street and then, in an act of pure braggadocio, completed the getup with a white snap-brim Bogey hat from Tripler. Out of sight! One day, when I arrived thus attired at the ballpark, Clancy, the manager, stopped me with a puzzled look on his big face. "You got a shoulder kink, Buzz?" he asked. "You're walking kinda crooked. Maybe you need an hour in the whirlpool bath, hunh?"

I blushed and straightened up, assuring him I was all right. But I knew what had happened. My old Capote crouch, the one I affected so assiduously in my youth, had come back upon me. A good omen indeed!

Friday night before my Monday, Buck Willis, my roomie,

and I drove up to Yaddo. It was after ten when we arrived, however, and a surly gatekeeper barred our way. "All the typewriters is locked up for the night," he muttered. "All the writers, too. Besides, I can't go around letting just any old hack in here." Disappointed, we saved something from the journey by circling through Bread Loaf, where a kindly lady who teaches Middle English at Mount Holyoke allowed me to loosen up on her big Remington. I worked out for an hour, testing old muscles. My motion was good, but I wasn't hitting the space bar with the old confidence.

I was ready when Monday morning came. I arose feeling refreshed, aware of a faint tremor in the backs of my knees, but grateful, on the whole, that *der Tag* had arrived. Then, as I stood in front of my mirror, making last adjustments to my uniform, my heart gave a great leap of dismay. I had no Fowler! It was a shocking oversight on my part. I could not turn up at the *Dijon Review* and confess to such an omission, and I was only too aware that no editor willingly lends his Fowler, even to an officemate who is trying to break out of a slump. That is one of the oldest superstitions in the game. I grabbed the telephone and called Lefty Kolb, our team's affable knuckle-baller. "Listen, Lefty," I said, spilling out the words in my haste, "have you got an old Fowler you could lend me for the day?"

"A what?" he said sleepily.

"A Fowler's *Modern English Usage*. Any edition will do, but I've got to have it right away."

"Gee, no, Buzz," he said. "I happen to know, because I was looking for mine only last week. I'm sorry as hell."

I thanked him, hung up, and hurried out to see if I could buy the volume. But no bookstores were open at that early hour. I had to settle for a Little Golden Dictionary, purchased from a drugstore. I carried it under my arm all day, hoping my temporary colleagues would accept it as a personal literary eccentricity.

"Editors' entrance?" I inquired, standing outside an open door in the dim third-floor corridor. I could feel my heart thumping under my buckskins.

"It's the only door we got," said the young man sitting inside, not lifting his eyes from his *Daily News.*

I entered, removed my hat, and extended my hand. "Ty Cobb," I said, employing the amusing sobriquet we had agreed upon at *Sports Illusory.* "I'm sort of working here today."

"I heard," the man said, giving me a soft, dry handshake. "I'm Eric." He had a skimpy mustache under an enormous haystack of unkempt blond hair, and I noticed that he wore purple socks and a pair of cracked patent-leather pumps.

The room was littered with newspapers, disorderly piles of letters—bills, by the look of them—and empty cardboard containers of coffee. There was a standing screen to my left, and from behind this I heard the low hum of voices and the clink of teacups in the next room. These scholarly sights and sounds unmanned me for a moment. "Look," I said to Eric. "Can I warm with you for a few minutes? Before I go in there?"

"O.K.," he said indifferently. "But I'm just the office boy around here."

We warmed for ten minutes, tossing aphorisms and capping easy quotations. I began to feel better, and I ventured a pitch I had used with some success in college. "Isn't it curious," I said, "that neither Cowley nor Trilling has observed that the watery images in the final sentences of both *A Farewell to Arms* and *Tender Is the Night* are direct, if unconscious, inheritors of a lineage tracing back to the closing passages of *Moby Dick,* in which the *Pequod* slips beneath those tiresomely symbolic waves? It's a curious lacuna in our critical thesaurus."

The effect of this upon Eric was unexpected. He straightened up and glared at me angrily. "Watch that stuff," he said bitterly. "No rhetorical questions without you give me a warning, see? Watch that showboating, busher."

"Oh, sure," I said, abashed. "Sure, sure, sure. I'm sorry. Anything you say."

I was now ready; the hour had come. Eric led me into the back room, and I introduced myself awkwardly. I recognized most of the faces, of course; as a boy, I had pasted their likenesses, clipped from Sunday book-review sections, inside my locker door. Blevins Carroll, the editor, was seated at a high old-fashioned roll-top desk, his great forehead gleaming palely above a green eyeshade. Morgan MacPhee and Hastings Latrobe, the devastating, heavily bearded pair recently purchased from *Partisan Review* in exchange for five British critics and an undisclosed amount of cash, were bent over the morning *Times*, working the crossword puzzle together. A fourth figure was stretched out on an old cot against one wall, his head buried in his arms. From time to time, he groaned. Too much *espresso* the night before, I guessed privately. The first three acknowledged my presence with curt nods. I was aware of a professionalism, a true, burning intolerance, in this room, and I knew happily that I would not encounter any false bonhomie here today. These men were admitting me to their company as an equal, with all the cynical hostility of the élite.

Thus encouraged, I began to take careful note of details—material to flesh out my narrative for *Sports Illusory*. I perceived that although Blevins Carroll talked out of the right side of his mouth, he wrote with his left hand, a tremendous defensive advantage in an editor who is also a novelist. (Most editors are right-handed.) Like all true intellectuals, these men smoked cigarettes. There were open packs all over the room, in pockets and on desks, within reach of limber, preoccupied fingers. Intellectuals light their cigarettes with matches, never lighters, striking flame with a single, deft inward motion, and usually throwing the used match stubs on the floor. I noted that the members of the staff usually addressed each other by their first names, only rarely employing such alternatives as "old chap" or "fella." This fact, in turn, led me to a further discovery: many critics have first names that are more customarily surnames—Blevins, Morgan, Hastings, and so forth. This gives them a superiority in bylines almost from birth.

"Well, we might as well get to it," Carroll said at last. He leaned forward and tossed me a thick, untidy sheaf of manuscript. "Anything here we should use?" he asked.

I licked my lips. I was aware that the three were watching me closely. I looked down at the manuscript. It had been scrawled, apparently with a blunt pencil, on flimsy sheets of pink paper. It was in a language I didn't recognize, but the varying length of the lines made me guess it was a piece of free verse. "Hmm," I said, stalling. "Well . . . Well, it isn't typewritten."

The three men looked at each other in surprise, exchanging smiles of apparent relief. "Yes," Latrobe said eagerly, "and we don't accept untyped submissions."

"I never thought of that!" MacPhee said.

"And he didn't enclose any return postage," Carroll added. He took the manuscript from me and dropped it in a wastebasket. "Nice work, Mr. Cobb," he said, looking at me with new respect.

Alas, it was not to remain as easy as that. Overconfident, working too fast, I soon found myself making the simplest anti-intellectual blunders. I voted against a film review, a reëvaluation of Bugs Bunny as the American *Übermensch*, on the ground that it was frivolous. Carroll snatched it back angrily, stating that it would probably be the lead article in their next issue. "Don't you know Warner Brothers cartoons are way, way in, man?" he said. Then I voted *for* an essay on the nursery years of Samuel Beckett, which struck me as fresh and amusing. "Pap!" Carroll snorted. "*Kitschy*-koo," Latrobe muttered. The figure on the couch shuddered at my obtuseness. A terrible exhaustion flowed over me. I was in deep waters, far over my head.

At this juncture, Eric's face appeared around the side of the screen. "Omnescu is here for his interview," he announced.

For a moment, my nerve failed me utterly. Tired, flustered, my ill-conditioned critical reflexes already screaming in protest, I was now to face the most feared literary slugger of our time.

Omnescu, the free-swinging Rumanian avant-gardist, author of three volumes of *haiku* written in classical Etruscan, was about to take part in one of the *Dijon Review*'s famed interviews-in-depth, and *I* was expected to lead our team's assault. "No, no!" I cried weakly. "It's too much to ask. I can't go on. These bone chips in my writing hand . . ."

"Courage, Cobb," Latrobe whispered in my ear. "We'll be here behind you, fielding the answers. Just lay your searching questions down the middle."

Well, I tried. I'll say that for myself in retrospect. When the great man had been ushered in and seated in a broken armchair, I cleared my throat and forced myself to look at his fearsome visage rising above his filthy turtleneck sweater and huge shoulders like an angry winter moon over a range of mountains. His cold zircon eyes, which I had seen heretofore only from a seat in the back rows of the Y.M.H.A. Poetry Center auditorium, now fixed themselves on me with horrid anticipation. I thought confusedly of my success with the foreign manuscript, and stammered out, "Mr. Omnescu, do you, uh, write with a p-pencil?"

To my astonishment, he popped a soft answer straight back to my teammates. "Hah!" he said. "Axcellant qvastion. Axcellant! Until last year, Omnescu writes always with pancil. But last January, with Guggenheim money, Omnescu buys electric typewriter. Results: electric!" And for the next ten minutes he chatted warmly about his rapport with a writing device so happily symbolic of our depersonalized milieu, while the editors scribbled busily and gratefully in their notebooks.

Unfortunately, I was now so emboldened that I decided on another change-up pitch. It was to be my last effort of the day. "Sir," I said, "have you read and been influenced by Yogi Berra's autobiography?"

His face turned red, then purple. "Yoga!" he exploded. "You ask me—Omnescu—about yoga? That qvackery? You vaste my time with meesticism, with Indian gymnastics for housewives on nut diets? Omnescu will put you straight on yoga, you meeserable counter-intellactual." Spluttering, jabbering incoherently, lapsing frequently into his native tongue, he launched on a monologue so verbose and so rambling that long before he had finished, Carroll and MacPee and Latrobe had dropped their pencils out of sheer ennui.

"That'll be all," Carroll said to me crisply. He beckoned to Eric to take my place in the circle of chairs. I had been relieved again. I was washed up in this league.

Weeping, I dropped my Little Golden Dictionary and stumbled out and down the stairs toward the street. I had forgotten my Bogey hat, but I knew I would never need it again. Dejected, sore of head and spirit, I trudged slowly toward the subway. Then, just before I reached the corner, my glance fell upon two ragged urchins in my path. They were bent over, unaware of me, writing busily with chalk on the pavement. Their scrawled words stretched the entire width of the sidewalk, from curb to building front.

"Hey, Jim-mee!" one of them yelled. "Watch me, Jim-mee! Watch me write. I'm William Styron, Jim-mee! "I'm Styron writing!"

"Go-wann!" the other called back, scribbling excitedly. "Lookit me, Billy. Watch *me* write! *I'm* Elizabeth Hardwick!"

Touched, deeply moved by these innocent gamins, I blew my nose and began to cheer up. "The game will go on," I whispered to myself. "Even without me, it will go on. The great American pastime will never die."

More Film Fun

(Tentative Program Notes for Another Week of High
Cinematic Entertainment, Drawn Up After a Study
of the Festival News from Lincoln Center)

The Peapod Bowl (*Atafumu*)

In a dazzling, deeply significant switch from the decadent
opulence that marked his *Deacon Watanabe and the Shower
Clogs* and the rustic crudity of his *The Rice Splitter* (winner
of the Grand Prix at the 1968 McKeesport Festival), Protubo
Mitihara has gone to the contemporary half-world of the Osaka
bowling alleys to bring us a disquieting, understated, and un-
lovely tale of a teen-age pinspotter who is suffering from a crisis
of identity brought on by the threat of automation. The symbol-
ism here (the round perfection of the bowling balls marred
by ugly yet necessary finger holes) is pervasive yet never blatant.
Henry Mancini has composed a brilliant score that combines
the harsh thunder of falling tenpins with the classic tinkling
dissonances of Japanese folk opera. You will especially remember
the painful eleven-minute sequence, played in total silence and
darkness, in which Zenzu Fumita, in the role of the hero's
uncle, gropes for the light switch in the men's room.

Paddle Your Own Canoe (*Pas de le Rhône que Nous*)

It was inevitable, given the long Gallic fascination with *Le Far
Ouest*, that Jean-Paul Luc would eventually fashion a film
out of Cooper's *Leatherstocking Tales*, but who would have

guessed that his freehand cinematic translation would trans-
form Chingachgook into a middle-aged, sexually repressed Miche-
lin restaurant scout (Jean-Paul Poulenc), or that Natty Bumppo
would emerge as Natalie Beaupré, a shy yet smoldering Girl Scout
leader (Jeanne-Paule Morbideau) who loses first her compass
and then her virginity during a hike in the Bois de Boulogne?
This film, frankly prurient, never escapes into easy sentimental-
ism, and though some in the audience may be shocked by the
filling-station scene or the episode of the *marrons glacés*, none
will deny that Luc's cinematographic intelligence has brought
us a fresh comprehension of the "innocence" of the great American woods.

Nibbles

The National Film Board of Canada, which has been respon-
sible for some of the best documentaries in recent years (its
vivid *Hockey Puck Injuries* won second prize at the Ottawa
Biennale), has surpassed itself with this unflinching study of nail-
biting habits in a typical middle-income household. Although
Director Tony Garwood and Producer Al Gurtch stick manfully
to their subject while depicting, with brisk crosscutting, the slow
decline of parental confidence suffered by teen-agers with low
cuticle resistance, the real hero of the film is downtown Saska-
toon, a *mise en scène* of surprising beauty and ambivalence.
This masterpiece proves again that subject matter is no obstacle,
and almost of no concern, to modern cinematic genius.

The Groans of Winter (*Vintersgrönen*)

This rare print of Gunnar Malmstrom's much-whispered-about
early chef-d'œuvre offers a first chance for American audiences
to see an uncut version of a film from the Swedish master's
pre-religious period. The movie, which has been banned for
more than a decade in Spain and Jersey City, deals with the
progressive alienation, aberration, and madness of a young
Stockholm eel-sorter after he surprises his mother and his aged

tutor together in a sauna bath. Shot mainly with a handheld and defective 16-mm. camera, it contains crude, juvenile versions of Malmstrom's purposefully "tiresome" repeated symbols, juxtapositions, and allegorical leitmotivs, and as such is of inestimable cinematohistorical value. And, as Henry Miller has said, "This film is not *just* about lust and insanity. It is also a wet fish in the face to all those who would deny the delicacy of the human spirit."

Once Again Chapatties (*Chapatty, Chapatty, Chapatty*)

Has Indian farce been done to death? Certainly not! Once again the puckish Ram Mukerjee has dug deep into his inexhaustible bag of cinematic magic tricks and wry ironies to bring us this heartwarming tragicomedy about a Hindu family struggling to find its multiple identity against the age-old handicaps of illiteracy, matriarchy, monkey worship, and boredom. On the surface, this leisurely, 210-minute epic merely recounts the effects of a crippling strike at the local paraldehyde works upon a small north-Indian mud village, but woven through this coarse fabric are bright threads of allegory and impudence that ask profound questions about the direction and meaningfulness of our Western agrarian policies. On the same bill, there will be a fifty-minute short that depicts, with utter frankness and in fantastic colors, the sinuous dalliance and courtship habits of the oarfishes of the Great Barrier Reef; the musical accompaniment, singularly apt, is by the Vienna Boys' Choir.

Little Men

At last, the public will have an opportunity to make up its own mind about the merits of this filmic *cause célèbre*! Does this eleven-minute, 8-mm. entry constitute "an exceptionally faithful, heartbreaking, and utterly poetic rendering of the ancient myth of Bellerophon and Pegasus," as it has been characterized by film historian and curator Fermin Terwilliger, who accidentally came upon a print in the back room of a rare book and film emporium on Sixth Avenue? Or is it, in the words of its surprised creator, Sergei (Blue Serge) Eisenstein, "Just another piece of schlocky beefcake"? Mr. Eisenstein, whose other credits include *Mondo Hondo, A Streetcar Named David,* and *The Wedding of the Member,* also disclaims any connection between the well-known Louisa May Alcott novel and his own classic of the same name, which depicts with utter frankness a startling simultaneous search for identity by three jockeys in the steam-room of a West Coast Y.M.C.A.

The Mars Wheel

The only other American entry in this festival is of the new, hard-line, super-realistic Hollywood genre, as insistent and electrifying as a Dexedrine tablet. This drama, set in the America of the day after tomorrow, deals with a frightening power struggle that ensues when the paranoid top magnate of a vast car-rental agency attempts to seize control of the National Aeronautics and Space Administration, thus blackmailing Congress into a repeal of the corporate income-tax statutes. The gripping climax, all the more convincing for its unlikelihood, comes when the C.I.A. must track down the Chief Executive's purloined credit card in time to abort a doomed billion-dollar Mars shot. Omar Sharif easily "steals" the acting honors with his bijou portrayal of the Minority Whip.

Oogu (*Oogu*)

Even the most dedicated film enthusiast might hesitate at the prospect of sitting through a three-hour movie that deals with an eighty-five-year-old Eskimo grandmother who suffers from psychopathic fear of the cold and who is exiled, toothless, to the Husky pens after a lifetime of honorable boot-chewing. But doubters will think twice when they learn that this haunting, blizzard-swept drama comes from the hand of Luigi Da-Rimini, creator of the triumphant, lusty *Saltimbocca* (winner of the Prix-Fixe at the Pomfret School Festival). DaRimini's patient, unwinking camera and an untranslated, undubbed sound track that is alive with Eskimo gutturals and canine snarls combine, however slowly, to bring alive a relationship between the old woman, the lead dog, and a herd of unseen caribou, that is pure Genet. Klikiat Ipaka, the aged heroine, establishes herself in this, her first film, as an actress of impenetrable subtlety. Not to be missed!

Shorts Unlimited!

Almost everybody is making films these days, and this closing day's program is a potpourri of shorter recent works that illustrates the unlimited new horizons of the medium. Among the forty-seven featurettes are *The Trial, Conviction, and Execution of Chicken-Licken,* a film conceived, acted, directed, and shot in its entirety by Miss Hyssop's second graders' workshop in Azuza, California; and *Innies and Outies,* a sensitive nature study produced by the Florida Navel-Orange Growers Co-op. In an altogether different vein is *O Quel Cruller!*—at first glance a rather far-fetched nudie farce, which turns out to be a clever new rendering of the annual stockholders' report of the Mother Rappaport Bagel & Doughnut Corp. Here too is *Amoebophrenia,* a short combining microphotography and cartoon doodling (a process developed by the Rockefeller Institute Film Workshop), which explicates, with wacky interpolated dialogue, the loss of identity sensed by an amoeba as it undergoes binary fission. Finally, mention must be made of Anders Mickoszy's *Bottle Fatigue* (winner of the Silver Potato at the Boise Festival), a stunningly arrayed montage of abandoned bedsprings, old bottle caps, and broken glass, which says more about the slow poison of prejudice and the new strides being made by Human Encounter groups than a dozen weighty books of sociology! The utter silence in the audience during the running of this two-reeler and the relieved applause at its termination are a tribute to its high seriousness—and to the maturity of the cinema art in our time.

Turtletaub and
the Foul Distemper

The facts concerning last winter's mystifying New England airplane accident—referred to variously in the press as the "Vanishing Pilot Case" or the "Pancaked Jetliner Puzzle"— are so fresh in the public mind that I hesitate to reopen the matter, lest I be found guilty of second-hand sensationalism. Yet the truth, or as much of it as perhaps we will ever know, deserves to be set forth, if only because it forms part of a far darker and more tangled tale that certain authorities wish to suppress. Foremost among these is my old friend Inspector Turtletaub, of the Special Assignments Bureau, who first told me the whole story and yet who now claims concern for my health and whimpers that "the world is not ready" for the terrible truth. Lies, lies! My health has never been better—ha, ha!—and here, sipping champagne high above the Atlantic as I fly eastward to a new life, I pick up my pen and prepare to set down nothing less than a true history. I defy you, Lionel Turtletaub, to deny a syllable of it!

The details of the accident are easily set forth in précis. On a stormy March afternoon, a regularly scheduled airliner bound for Boston radioed the Logan tower to report a sudden failure of all navigational and directional instruments, as well as an undiagnosed and uncorrectable loss of power. The plane, in short, was lost and on the point of making a forced landing. This was the last radio contact. At 5:07 P.M. (E.S.T.), the inhabitants of Burbage Fens, Mass., a small village near Athol, heard the noise of a plane circling in low-lying clouds directly overhead—a roar that was abruptly silenced as the plane seemed to go into the ground in the environs of the Presumptionist Brothers monastery on a hillside just north of town. Hurrying there, the alarmed villagers were relieved to find the plane not only intact but entirely undamaged. The pilot, it could be seen, had made a brilliant wheels-up landing on the lawn of the monastery, formerly a large private estate. The monks, who had been at table in their refectory, were now trying to pry open the airliner's cabin doors. When they did so, they found the fifty-three passengers, the co-pilot, the engineer, and three stewardesses still strapped in their seats. None, it was quickly determined, had suffered so much as a bump or a scratch, yet all fifty-eight of them were semiconscious. Moaning and shuddering, sometimes crying out in evident horror, they were quickly removed to a nearby hospital, where they were found to be suffering from shock. Recovery was rapid, and within twenty-four hours all of the survivors were released. To this day, however, not one of them has ventured a word of explanation as to the circumstances of the crash; if pressed by relatives or reporters, they grow pale, tremble uncontrollably, and make piteous attempts to leave the room. The findings of the National Transportation Safety Board have never been released. Nor has any information been given as to the whereabouts of the pilot, Captain Sebastian Moran, or of one of the monks, a novice known as Brother Larry, neither of whom has been seen since the moment of the crash.

There, as far as the public knows, the matter stands—just where it stood that evening six weeks ago when Inspector Turtletaub finished his press briefing and the last reporters, still muttering their complaints and questions, had been led from his office. The last, that is, save I. Turtletaub looked up from his desk and saw me still in my accustomed chair.

"Didn't you hear me, Humberstone?" he growled. "That's all. There's the door."

"I heard you, Lionel," I said. I walked over to the door and snapped the lock. Then I threw my pencils and copy-paper into the wastebasket. Then I held open my jacket for his inspection. "No visitors, no notes, no tapes," I said. "Now, Lionel, off the record. . . ."

He rose and passed his hands nervously over his towering forehead. "I'd like to, Humberstone," he said unhappily. "But this, believe me, is a case like no other. It must remain forever veiled."

"Lionel," I said reproachfully. "This is me, Walt Humberstone—or rather, I. Have I ever violated a confidence?"

"You don't *understand!*" he burst out. "It's you I must protect, along with everybody else. Everyone out there!" He made a sweeping gesture with one hand. "They're not strong enough—*nobody* is strong enough to hear this!"

I smiled. "Remember the Shopworn Torso case?" I said. "Remember the Hoboken Glutton? I helped you with those, Lionel. I'm a tough old newshawk, so leave my feelings out of this. You've been on this case for weeks now, and I can see what it's doing to you. What was it—a new kind of hijack? Nerve gas, maybe? Weathermen? When will you make a collar?"

He shook his head again, threw himself into his chair, and then jumped up and resumed pacing. "No arrests, no arrests," he muttered to himself. "They're gone. Two twisted minds like that, once again loosed on the world. . . . Who would believe it?"

"*I'd* believe it, Lionel," I said gently.

"Very well!" he cried, once more flinging himself behind his desk. "But remember—you begged me. Don't blame me later!" He took a bunch of keys from his side pocket, unlocked a drawer in his desk, and drew forth a bulging file.

"You said 'two twisted minds,'" I said. "Do you mean that the pilot and the monk were in it together?"

"Yes, of course," Turtletaub said, ruffling papers.

"But the monk was on the ground."

"Exactly. The co-pilot's evidence was perfectly clear about that. Seventeen passengers on the right-hand side of the plane confirmed his report. As the plane slithered across the lawn on its belly, the monk, later said to be 'Brother Larry,' ran forward from under a tree and seemed to be struck down by the right wingtip. They could all see him lying there as the plane stopped."

"But that sounds as if the monk was—" I began.

"Was *waiting* for the plane, yes," the Inspector said excitedly. "Was 'in it' with the pilot, yes. Was a joint planner and principal in a plot of truly diabolical premeditation! Was a criminal impostor of monstrous patience and cunning! Was, in short, a match for his partner in evil, the rascally Captain 'Sebastian Moran.' Ah, my friend, the arrogance of that name! The deranged brilliance of it!" He broke off and shook a sheaf of papers in my face. "They are the same pair!" he said fiercely. "The pattern is all to clear. Brother Larry is the North Woods Barrymore, and Captain Moran is the Mad Editor. They have struck again!"

"What?" I cried, utterly dumbfounded now. "Who? When? Where?"

Inspector Turtletaub looked at me musingly. "Where shall we begin, Humberstone?" he said. "These are very deep waters."

He began, a few minutes later, with the Moses Paulding disappearance. I remembered the story—a minor mystery of a decade before. Moses Paulding, a respectable advertising account executive, had vanished after a cocktail party in Darien, where he lived. There had been a fracas of some kind. Paulding had walked out, never to be seen again.

"Moses Paulding," Turtletaub told me, "was suffering from Retardate Wildeanism, which means that he was never able to think of clever remarks until too late, usually the next morning. This is a commonplace ailment—we all have it to some degree—but Paulding's was a bad case. He was known in Darien as something of a dullard, yet at home in bed at night or while shaving the next morning, he would suddenly burst out laughing as he thought of some flashing riposte, some edged apothegm, to throw into a conversation already hours or days dead. One day while driving in his car alone, he thought of a bon mot concerning Angela Thirkell, the English novelist, and was so convulsed that he had to pull over to the median strip to compose himself. That evening, he told his wife the joke—she filled me in on all this, much later—and explained to her that he had resolved to remember this one until it was needed. He planted it in his memory, so that he would be able to pluck it forth, casually and elegantly, at the very first mention of Angela Thirkell at somebody's dinner table or poolside party. The trouble was, of course, that Angela Thirkell wasn't exactly the best-known author in Darien. Oh, one may suppose that a few of his neighbors had heard of her or read her, but it wasn't a name that came up every day."

"Still isn't," I said, yawning.

"Very well," Turtletaub said, eying me. "*Bref*, nobody mentioned Angela Thirkell. There was our friend Paulding preparing his one little firecracker before every dinner party and sociable—fondling and polishing it in his pocket, so to speak—and no one would light the fuse. Five years went by, and no Thirkell. She even died in that time, but no one in Darien noticed it or mentioned the fact in front of Paulding. The poor fellow was going mad. He'd almost forgotten, and then, kismet!—he was a guest at a large summer lawn party when suddenly he thought he heard the magic sound of 'Angela Thirkell' drift through the evening air. The voice he'd heard was at the opposite end of a ninety-seven-foot veranda, but Paulding dropped his drink, left the people he was with, and ran all the way over there, shoving through the other guests and upsetting a tray of sandwiches on the way. When he got there, it turned out to be a group of visitors who were total strangers to him—and the name they had dropped, by the way, was Studs Terkel, not Angela Thirkell—but Paulding pushed his way right in among them, and then, still panting but trying to appear offhand and debonair, he said, 'Well, *I've* always thought Angela Thirkell was a thquare.'"

"What!" I said, sitting up in my chair.

"That's what *they* said," said the Inspector. "They made

him repeat it, the poor, doomed soul, and this time the whole party, easily sixty or seventy people, was listening, and nobody laughed. Nobody said a word, in fact. And at that instant, we may safely speculate, the mind of Moses Paulding cracked apart, like a dropped fingerbowl. He walked slowly down the veranda steps and up the slate path to the driveway, and then turned and faced them. He lifted both his arms, and in a hair-raising, keening voice he cried, 'Revenge shall be miii-nnne!' He left, and no one has seen him—at least, under *that* name— to this day."

"Serves him right," I said, rubbing my burning temples. "But what about the plane? What about—"

Turtletaub held up his hand, consulted another file, poured himself a sip of water from his decanter, and resumed. "Time: seven years ago," he said. "Place: a certain village in northern-most Quebec, well above Chicoutimi. The only inhabitants are trappers and lumberjacks, with the exception of the monks resident in a large local monastery. The only newspaper—"

"*Another* monastery?" I said.

"You've the makings of a detective, my good fellow," said the Inspector. "Yes. And the only newspaper is a modest bilingual weekly called *L'Éclaireur du Muskeg*. Properly modest, because there is normally no news whatsoever in this godforsaken com-pound—no arrivals, no departures, few females, few diver-sions. The only excitement, in fact, is the annual stage presenta-tion performed by the inhabitants of the monastery. This play is a regionally famous institution—or has been ever since its management was put entirely into the hands of a monk named—" He paused and consulted his notes. "Yes. Father Marcel Squegg."

"Funny name," I said.

"No," said Turtletaub grimly. "Not funny in the least. Well, Squegg, we have learned, was a first-class theatrical direc-tor and actor, an enthusiastic *metteur en scène* who succeeded in involving every one of his fellow ecclesiastics in the annual mumming. There was a different presentation each autumn—

one year a farce, the next a musical, the next Shakespeare, and so forth. Whatever its nature, Squegg directed, handled the casting and lighting, and played the leading role. He was brilliant, and his foremost supporter and press agent was the local newspaper, which, curiously enough, was also written and edited and printed entirely by one man, a friend of Squegg's."

"The Mad Editor!" I whispered. "And the North Woods Barrymore!"

"Exactly. Thus the editor dubbed him in the newspaper after Squegg's *succès fou* as Hamlet one year. He gave the monk the entire front page—photographs, headlines, and the better part of the rave notice. Unsurprisingly, such news quickly spread across the province, and soon word—the expected word— came up from the diocese, which permitted Squegg to put into motion the final details of the plan. He was summoned in by the abbot and reminded of the sin of pride. He was ordered to continue as director of forthcoming plays but was enjoined from further stardom. Squegg, of course, consented to abase himself. Well, the next year's item of repertory was a full-scale revival of *Uncle Tom's Cabin*, and the customary sellout complement of woodsy first-nighters turned out to cheer their local Garrick—only to find his name absent from the bill. Squegg was in the play, in fact, but was not noticed, for he had cast himself as one of the dogs that follow Eliza across the ice in the melodramatic chase scene. He was completely encased in a bloodhound costume and was not recognized when he went sniffing and baying across the stage."

"I hope the play was better than this story," I said irritably. "This is the stupidest—"

"We'll see who's stupid!" Turtletaub snapped. "You are now in precisely the same position as those poor, helpless reubens. The Mad Editor and that fiendish priest have you at their mercy, and you don't even know it." He extracted a faded newspaper clipping from his file. "Here is the story about *Uncle Tom's Cabin* that appeared in the *Éclaireur* the next morning. Never mind the review—just read the headline."

It was a banner right across the top of the page, and I read it out loud: " 'père squegg in hound rôle.' "

Turtletaub stooped and retrieved the clipping, which had fluttered from my fingers. I was at his desk, emptying the decanter over my head.

"The newspaper office was sacked that same morning," he went on. "The townspeople tore the place apart. By that time, of course, Paulding and the priest had long since departed, having made good their departure under cover of darkness. Paulding, we now know, was the editor. They were in it together, right from the start. We don't know where they met, of course, but we do know who Squegg was and how he got that way."

"No!" I spluttered. *"Please*, no. I don't want to hear about it. Nix."

Inexorably, he reached for another file and went on. "Originally, a Father Martin Quist, an unremarkable young priest in a poor Midwest parish," he intoned. "So poor, in fact, that they had to let out some of the rooms in the rectory to boarders, in order to make ends meet. Well, this was well back in the fifties, in the unlamented McCarthy era, and soon ugly stories were afloat to the effect that one of the boarders was a Communist and possibly an atheist. Parish morale declined and suspicions were rife, and one Sunday Father Quist determined to put an end to the matter. He arose in the pulpit after Mass—"

I put my hands up, as if to ward off a blow.

"—and told the congregation that there was nothing in it. The accused boarder, he said, was not a Catholic, but he certainly wasn't a Communist or an atheist. 'In fact,' he told them, holding back a smile, 'I can assure you that we have nothing here but an unconfirmed roomer.' " Turtletaub flicked me a glance. "Maybe I should spell that out for you," he said. "He meant—"

"I *know* what he meant!" I said, gagging. "A man like that— Why, I would have— Excommunication!"

"Not quite," said the Inspector, "but he was out of office

and out of the parish by nightfall. Exile and Squeggdom ensued. Before he left town, you see, he, too, made a public vow of revenge. Exactly like Paulding."

"Which brings your story full circle," I said, rising hastily and grabbing for my raincoat. "And a terrible story it's been, too. Well, thanks, Lionel, and—"

"*Sit down!*"Turtletaub thundered. "We haven't even come to the plane crash yet. And you asked for this—remember?"

The next hour dragged by painfully as the Inspector described his own involvement in the case—the urgent request for his services, first from the Canadian Mounties, then by Interpol; the months of careful backtracking and painstaking police work that uncovered the identities of the two lunatics; and the fears, kept very secret, of forensic medical experts that the Paulding-Quist syndrome might prove in some way to be contagious, thus threatening the Western mind with a truly terrifying new madness. These fears, in fact, were deepened by the number of parallel cases that distracted Turtletaub from his manhunt. There were indeed other victims of the foul distemper, and Turtletaub, in his methodical manner, spared me none of the details.

"Now, you take the Lord Tweedy business, back in '65," he said. "That certainly *sounded* like Paulding's work. A shocking tale. A wealthy British tourist had arrived in a little Alpine village one afternoon, where he joined a crowd of local citizens watching a burning chalet. Could he have *lit* that fire? Possibly. We shall never know. As the flames died down, he observed quietly that it was rather early in the season to see Swiss charred. The man hadn't counted on the multilingual capacities of the natives, for by the time I arrived in the Bernese Oberland, two days later, all traces of his corpse had been eradicated. We suspect that he lies at the foot of the Reichenbach Fall. Only a study of his signature in the register at the local inn convinced me that he could not have been Paulding. Can you hear me down there?"

I was lying under his desk, with my head partially concealed in his overturned wastebasket, and I waved one hand feebly to indicate continuing consciousness.

"Similarly," Turtletaub continued, "the tragic affair of the Black Retainer *could* have been Quist-Squegg's work—or so I believed when I first investigated. The difficulty of playing a Negro butler with sufficient servile aplomb as to take in the entire Culpepper family, as well as all the other plantation hands, is a challenge that would attract a great actor. Surely you remember the case—it led to the overnight revival of sixteen Klan chapters in South Carolina alone. My investigations on the scene, however, proved the unlikelihood of premeditation, and I had to absolve our two loonies of any involvement. To be sure, the aged retainer knew that his master, Colonel Gaylord Culpepper, was a hopeless alcoholic who regularly did away with fourteen mint juleps before lunchtime, but how could he have anticipated that on that particular day the Colonel, in stumbling search of another bottle of bourbon, would pass out in the pantry, crashing headlong in a welter of comestibles? And how could he have arranged matters so that, in his fall, the Colonel would pull down upon himself a two-pound, economy-size box of Hershey's Instant Cocoa? No, it was pure accident, and the missing butler—who has so far escaped apprehension—was but a chance victim suddenly struck down by this sinister new affliction. His mistress, you see, noting the absence of the family rumhound from the environs of the decanter, rang the bell, and when the courtly servitor had shuffled into the room she said, 'Cudjo, wheah's the Colonel?' How the poor fellow must have trembled as he saw the pit suddenly yawn at his feet! He could not help himself. He bowed and murmured, 'Massa's in de cocoa grounds.' "

I sprang up from under Turtletaub's desk, conking my head on the typewriter table, and flew to the window. "Air!" I gasped, clawing at the latch. "Give me air!"

"Yes, the airplane," Turtletaub continued, closing his eyes

and forming a steeple with his fingers. "It's time to sum up. For all my efforts, Paulding-Moran and his evil partner remained undetected right up to the moment last month when their paths, by mad prearrangement, converged. Picture the drama. Paulding, in the pilot's seat, makes certain secret adjustments to the controls to destroy all navigational signals and diminish power. He alerts the passengers to their plight, and the 'lost' plane plummets toward its rendezvous on the hilltop. As the jet slithers across the grass, 'Brother Larry' bursts from hiding, dashes forward, and *pretends* to be struck down by the wing tip. The plane stops, the pilot coolly makes his report to the strapped-down passengers and crew, and, a moment later, he and his accomplice make good their escape, leaving half a hundred helpless victims in a condition of mass psycholepsy. *Finis.*"

"'*Finis*'?" I croaked. "But—but, what *happened*?"

Turtletaub looked at me for an instant, puzzled. "Oh," he said at last, "didn't I tell you before? After the plane stopped moving, Paulding turned on the plane's intercom and announced, "Well, folks, out of the flying plan and into the friar.' But, my dear fellow—" And with a troubled face he sprang toward me as I toppled forward gratefully into oblivion.

My champagne glass is empty; the plane dips toward Paris. My tale is nearly done. No need to recount the long, painful weeks of my illness, the battle for the cloudy fortress of my mind. Suffice it to say that while cleverly feigning coma one morning I overheard the rascally Turtletaub—that devoted "friend!" that defender of public weal!—plotting with a band of white-garbed quacks for my permanent sequestration! "I blame myself," the villain told them again and again. "I should have seen it coming."

What he should have seen coming was my escape, that very evening. What he could *never* have seen coming was my present guise, the nature of my forthcoming career, and—*hee, hee, hee!*—my name. Shall I offer you a peep at my passport? Very well—there! You start back in surprise. It cannot be, you think! Ah, but it is. Pray let me introduce myself—"Lionel Turtletaub," at your disposal.

Lionel Turtletaub, who, by means of certain cleverly dispatched and intercepted cables, will shortly begin tenure as a detective on loan to the Sûreté. There, with full access to criminal files, I shall find my first accomplice. A Chinese, a Malay perhaps—it doesn't matter; he need only be Oriental. Then, within weeks, I select my victim. Already I can see her—a pert Parisian widow, habituated to a certain elegance, perhaps a young vicomtesse. *Pauvre chérie,* she is soon to be troubled by a series of minor robberies. First a ring, then a brooch, then the *lavallière* once presented to her by the late vicomte himself. The police are called; a master detective, an American Maigret, comes forward to offer his services. Turtletaub to the rescue! There is another robbery, though, and then another. Madame is disconsolate, but M. l'Inspecteur vows to crack the case. He spends hours at her flat, examining fingerprints. A friend-liness, a genuine warmth, seems to deepen between them. He offers certain gallantries; blushing, she dismisses them.

Then, on a warm night, Madame hears a sound, sees a shadow. She sits up in bed and screams! Through the French window springs Turtletaub, *pistolet* in hand. The trap has been sprung. His flashlight darts here, there, then focusses on the closet. A scuffle, an oath, and then out from behind Madame's dresses comes the criminal, hands high in the air. Still keeping him covered, Turtletaub snaps on the bedroom lights. The robber is wearing silk slippers, a long queue, and an angry Mandarin scowl. M. l'Inspecteur smiles at his distraught client, who charmingly pulls the coverlet higher toward her chin. Bowing, Turtletaub murmurs, "At last, Madame, I have discovered the Chink in your armoire!"

The no-smoking light is on: Paris. Paulding, *cher maître!* Quist, *mon semblable!* Ye shall be revenged!

The Exegesis of St. Nick

(Another Frightful Bloodletting in the Back Alleys
of the *New York Review of Books*)

To the Editors:

Nothing could be more flattering to a scholar than to have
a work of his reviewed by so eminent an expert as Hermann
Kronstadt, but candor forces me to confess a total lack of
surprise when I discovered that Professor Kronstadt had in
fact barely bothered to read my little exegesis of "A Visit from
St. Nicholas" (*Clement Moore and the Pre-Keynesian Apocalypse*,
Pottawattamie A. & M. University Press, $15) but had chosen
instead merely to add some footnotes to his own tediously
celebrated post-Freudian studies of the sexually feudalistic sub-
stratum in American children's books—a lode that so clearly
ran out in the early chapters of his recent *Wynken, Blynken
and Nod's Narrenschiff: Anal Archetypes on a Sea of Guilt*. If
this were all, I would remain silent, for students of Victorian
Americana have long since discovered that Professor Kronstadt
thinks he has the horse-and-buggy Christmas safely locked away
in his own curious clinic; he is the Molochian lump of coal
that lies at the bottom of every young scholar's stocking. But
Herr Kronstadt has gone too far in his ill-tempered review
in your columns, for he has not only obdurately refused to
accept the *Ding an sich* of my modest postulates but has launched
on a course of reckless misinterpretation and misquotation
that I can only regard as intentional. To paraphrase his testy
penultimate aphorism ("If Bertrand Russell was not Hölderlin,
Dr. Swiggett is certainly not Karl Mannheim"), I would murmur

that though I am not Mannheim, Professor Kronstadt may be more of a Nietzsche than even he or Max Weber would care to admit!

To be specific, I did not not suggest, or even *fail* to suggest, that the "Mama in her kerchief and I in my cap" *mise en scène* contained a "swaddled, nunlike repression of Clement Moore's unacceptably ravening id." I would not agree with this irresponsible bit of wildfire hermeneutics even if I had thought of it myself. Careful readers of my book will remember that my only comments on these early lines of the poem were those expatiating upon the profound sadness of doomed *laissez-faire* capitalism as sounded in the "visions of sugarplums danced through their heads" (*die Entzauberung der Zuckerpflaume*, in my phrase) image; plus, a bit later, my chapter dealing with the unbidden but frighteningly intrusive noises emanating from the overworked New England textile factories, and the concomitant din of rising industrial Jacobinism, that break in upon the narrator's long Victorian sleep: "When out on the lawn there arose such a clatter . . ."

I think it is typical of Professor Kronstadt's well-known vendetta style of criticism that he should concentrate in his review upon my careless but entirely insignificant omission of Prancer from the list of the reindeer (why did I not omit the equally androgynous Cupid or Dancer, Herr Kronstadt?), while he neglects all mention of my fruitful *propositio*, first suggested to me by Dietrich Maltby at the Determinism Workshop of 1965, that "Dasher, Dancer, Prancer & Vixen/Comet, Cupid, Donder & Blitzen" are, in fact, evidence of Clement Moore's desperate need for economic reassurance and moral book-balancing in a time of stress, through the agency of the sudden arrival of two thinly disguised Wall Street law firms on his rooftop.

I have further reservations, equally documented, about Professor Kronstadt's anti-critical fugue, but I will suppress them, if only in deference to the happy season. These would include an anguished protest against his charge that I have "failed utterly to deal with Moore's infantilistic anti-Semitism as seen in the transliteration and apotheosis of 'that good Protestant clubman called St. Nicholas' out of the blatantly obvious paradigm of the Wandering Jew known as Claus"; I deal with precisely that problem in my footnote on the "he looked like a pedlar just opening his pack" simile, and later, at further length, in my discussion of the inflationary rise of St. Nick up the chimney after the dividend distribution on the hearth, and the mysterious but unmistakably Faginesque gesture "laying his finger aside of his nose." (J. S. W. Turgeon and P. Rabbitt both suggest that this digital kinesis descends from the Hasidic finger-ritual *yodh-zahim*, but I am dubious.) Professor Kronstadt evidently failed to read that far in my book. That failure, so typical of those who continue to refuse to come to terms with the giant problem of the undistributed middle, disqualifies him as a Leavisite, or even as a backwoods Hobbesian, and certainly as a critic worthy of your pages.

Geoffrey Palamore Swiggett

Pottawattamie A. & M. University
Cornflake, Iowa

Hermann Kronstadt *replies:*

I wish to apologize to Dr. Swiggett for my inadvertent attribution of the "swaddled, nunlike" repression of the oh-so-good sleeping burghers of poor Clement Moore's jingle to him. That fragment of deft scholarship was, in fact, contained in an assigned "My Holidays" theme by one of my freshman students here at Redwood Poly; the paper was lying on my desk at the time that I wrote my review, so the mistake, though risible, is perhaps understandable. Actually, it's a pity that such an insight was not in Dr. Swiggett's book, for it struck me as by far the keenest *aperçu* I had read of the work in question, and might have led our unhappy author to a more fructuous harvest of conclusions.

Dr. Swiggett's semi-hysterical objections to my review suggest the anxieties of a cloistered exegete when he happens on an unexpected work of pseudepigrapha. He seems to blame me, rather than himself, for his book, and I would remind him quietly that the ideological equivalent of double agency, however unwitting, is antiquated Hegelian dialectic. After reading his letter, I must conclude that what seemed to be a mere failure to see (Kant's *Nichtverstehen*) is, in fact, a terrified refusal to know. Dr. Swiggett is an economist, but even economists have an unconscious, as Eriksen and George Lichtheim have agreed. His pathetic insistence on the little string of leftover Lekachmanisms that so entangles his work does not constitute a reply to the perfectly cheerful suggestions I made about Clement Moore's dark night of the soul; those dancing sugarplums *are* prepubertal phantasies, for all that Dr. Swiggett, with the blankets pulled up to his nose, insists that they are Bryanesque bags of free silver!

Why doesn't Dr. Swiggett attempt to answer my questions? What is he afraid of? His jiggery-pokery about New England textile mills does not hide the fact that "When out on the lawn there arose such a clatter" can *only* have been inspired by the then newly invented lawnmower, and thus constitutes another unconscious recrudescence of the sexual machine, the phallic juggernaut, that so troubled the dreams of our grandparents. At the risk of repeating myself, I would point out to Dr. Swiggett that only a dangerously overburdened superego could keep him from accepting that "Away to the window I flew like a flash,/Tore open the shutters and threw up the sash./The moon on the breast of the new-fallen snow/Gave the luster of midday to objects below" all too vividly describes an imperfectly sublimated vision of marital divestiture and defloration—perhaps of a less healthy nature than that which Melanie Klein discovered in "The Eve of St. Agnes." Can his conveniently forgotten Prancer and his strangely flying law firms obfuscate the preorgasmic urgency of "Now Dasher, now Dancer, now Prancer and Vixen,/On Comet, on Cupid, on Donder and Blitzen!"? Come, come, Dr. Swiggett, this is the twentieth century! Please join us in the ranks of the *libérés*, who remember that, in Ferenczi's words, "Only confirmed Oedipals insist that the penalty for *la trahison des clercs* is life imprisonment." Or are you afraid to ascend "to the top of the porch, to the top of the wall" and then "dash away, dash away, dash away all!"?

In the spirit of the season, I will close by pointing out that I have certainly not refused to accept the *donnée* of Dr. Swiggett's clumsily wrapped but charming little hand-woven potholder. I wish only to suggest, to him and to your readers, that Great Granddaddy Clement Moore's familiar old mahogany whatnot casts some startling shadows when held up to the strong light of intelligence!

The Great Starch Debate

(The Author of *Six Crises* Begins the Long Climb
Upward from 1962)

My experience has taught me that the first step in facing a crisis
is the ability to recognize that the crisis does in fact exist. This
requires a cool head and considerable personal background
in crisis-recognition. Looking back on it now, I am certain
that no one in our group but I sensed that a full-scale crisis
was in the making on that warm evening, early in my campaign
for the governorship of my native state, when we returned to
our hotel and I discovered that my shirts had not come back
from the laundry. We had enjoyed a busy and deeply satisfying
day of campaigning in the upper San Fernando Valley. I had
made a number of hard-hitting points in thirteen separate
speeches, and from the emotional point of view I had had
the always enriching experience of shaking hands with hundreds
of folks who seemed decidedly pleased with the principles I
had made perfectly clear to them. It had been another mountain-
top experience, and after it was over, there was a distinct temptation for my campaign staff and me to relax momentarily and
indulge ourselves in the luxury of retrospection and self-con-
gratulation. My discovery, at this juncture, that my shirts had
not come up from the laundry was at first only an irritation.
I had exhausted my small personal stock of clean white shirts
in the previous few days on the road, and the hotel laundry
had made a firm commitment to me of delivery by 5 P.M.
I had made it entirely clear to them that I required a clean
shirt for that evening, when I was scheduled to address a
Republican Peach-Pickers' Rally and then to participate in

a brass-tacks public debate on the issue of water fluoridation in parochial schools. When a thorough search of my suite turned up no package of clean shirts, I knew I had to take decisive action. I got busy on the telephone, speaking in person first to the front desk, then to the laundry room. Were my shirts ready? If not, would they be ready within the next hour?

Answer: negative. No one appeared to know where my shirts were. I hung up.

My estimate of the situation sharpened. As I sat by the bedroom telephone, engaged in inner debate, Earl Mazo, Bill Key, Alvin Moscow, Don Hughes, Jim Bassett, and several other members of my team came in. They sensed that something was "up." I quickly spelled out the facts for them and asked them for their evaluations. I told them I wanted advice, not sugar-coating.

The gist of their group opinion was at first glance both sensible and attractive. They urged me to take the easy way, to ride with the punch. They pointed out that a search for the shirts and a full disclosure of the reasons for their disappearance could be time-consuming and, in the long run, frustrating. They outlined the potential political dynamite that could be touched off if some member of our press entourage got wind of any "scene" that might ensue if I determined to follow through personally and find my shirts in the hotel. Several opinions pinpointed the fact that I could still in all probability go out and buy a new shirt before the beginning of the evening schedule. At least two of my companions kindly offered to lend me one of their own clean shirts—a warm expression of personal loyalty that I still cherish. As far as content went, their advice was excellent.

Nevertheless, I asked them to leave me alone for a few minutes while I made a deeper evaluation. I explained to them that a leader must do more than count the noses of his advisers. Left alone, I realized that I would be fully pardoned if I came to the conclusion that the situation I faced lay in one of life's gray areas, where the easier decision was called for. But there were principles involved, and I knew that any man who shirked the inner struggle at a time like this was guilty of irresponsibility. I saw at once that this was a crisis of an entirely new kind. This was not simply a case of Nixon being inconvenienced by the carelessness of one hotel or one laundry. If I were to permit myself to be bluffed out at this stage, it would mean that a citizen was acquiescing to the inefficiencies that woolly-thinking apologists often declare to be an innate part of the American system. It would be a case of Nixon putting his tail between his legs and surrendering to bureaucracy. I could not in conscience take such a course and then go before the people as their candidate. My philosophy has always been to do what is right. My instinct in this case was to act, to find the shirts.

Once I saw the course I had to take, any tension I might have felt disappeared. Courage—that is, the absence of fear—comes from conviction. I had long since learned that the decision-making process—that is, thinking—is the most trying part of any crisis. Now that my mind was made up, I felt cool and ready for battle. But merely to be doubly sure, I put long-distance calls through to Herb Brownell, Tom Dewey, Allen Dulles, and Charlie Halleck. All of them concurred, in broad terms, with the wisdom of my decision, and Charlie added that I had again made him proud to be an American. Tom Dewey was most specific. "This is a matter you must decide for yourself, Dick," he stated.

I summoned my staff back into the room. Quickly I laid the program before them. We would act, I said, because we were on the right side. But we would act responsibly, after thorough preparation and with proper human respect for the workings of the hotel's administrative apparatus. I asked them to prepare the necessary background material I would require, including data on laundry operations in general in the Free World, average delivery time of shirts by non-private launderers, wages and working conditions enjoyed by union and non-union ironers and folders, and so forth. I asked them to have this material before me in fifteen minutes, which would allow me perhaps another fifteen minutes for a crash briefing and intensive homework before we swung into action. They hurried off eagerly, and then for the first time I allowed myself to relax for a moment and reflect on what curious but perennially stimulating encounters history continued to place before the man who had once, back in a plain boy's bedroom in Yorba Linda, allowed his modest daydreams to encompass only the possibility of one day making the high-school junior-varsity debating team. Now, as far as background was concerned, the stage was set for that encounter that the American press, with more enthusiasm than accuracy, was later to call the Great Starch Debate.

Accompanied by two of my aides, I stepped into the elevator, turned, and faced the front of the car. "Laundry room, please," I said in a firm voice. The operator stole a puzzled glance at me, but I looked straight ahead. As we went down, I took stock of my physical condition. I was a trifle edgy, my palms were damp, and there was an empty feeling in the pit of my stomach. I suppose some might say that I was "nervous," but by drawing on personal experience I was able to recognize and even welcome these signs for what they were—the symptoms of a normal man in descent in a fast elevator.

We alighted in the sub-basement and I strode directly through the doors of the laundry room. I was at once enveloped in clouds of steam, but my painstaking briefing had prepared me for this eventuality, and I did not hesitate. In spite of the steam and the hiss and roar of washers and pressing machines, I was able to single out my man, the laundry manager, at once. He was behind a counter, wearing a white undershirt and white trousers. I introduced myself, and we shook hands. While our aides grouped themselves around us in the manner prescribed by protocol and roughed out between them the substance of the conversations to come, I took stock of my man. He exuded an unmistakable impression of weariness and ennui. Here, I knew, was a powerful adversary—a hard-core laundry manager, steeled to complaints, magnificently trained in evasion.

I got off to a particularly good start by pointing out to him that his failure to deliver my shirts constituted a breach of contract. In effect, I told him, he had failed to live up to his end of one of those countless small but vital agreements that permit men of good will to function together in our increasingly complex world.

He feigned bewilderment. The delivery of shirts was not in his province, he stated—only their processing.

Instinctively, I knew I had to press my attack. I asked him if he ever had any difficulty sleeping at night if he knew that even one of his customers felt less than complete satisfaction with the laundry service that day. I roughed out for him a broad panoramic view of the operations of our vast mercantile system and its concomitant and essential service subdivision.

He seemed reluctant to debate the points I had raised. He pounded the counter and, with some vivid and distinctly non-diplomatic peasant adages, stated that I was adding to, rather than clarifying, our differences.

My intensive preparations allowed me to absorb and counter his attack without being thrown off balance. I knew that from the standpoint of temper control this would be the worst possible time for me to blow my stack. I decided to shift tactics. An "end run" was called for. I pointed out that while over fifty-one million American males owned white shirts the average per-capita ownership (including steelworkers) was still only 2.3 shirts each, a figure that did not allow for any slipups in the laundry-processing industry. *Time* magazine later characterized this as "a beefed-up riposte that scored heavily in the drama."

Now it was his turn to change the pace. Forcing a laugh, he asked me if I was not being guilty of obscurantism.

"That's not my way," I retorted. "I shall never be guilty of obscurantism."

He poked a pudgy finger at me. "We are capable of dialectics, too, you know," he said menacingly.

Now we were going at it hammer and tongs. I was vaguely

aware that a considerable crowd of laundresses, waiters, bell-boys, and house detectives had surrounded us. None of them had ever heard anything like this before behind the doors of their laundry room, and I knew that even if I failed now in my primary mission, my journey would not prove to have been entirely in vain.

At this moment, one of the manager's assistants pressed a note into his hand. We both paused, panting in the steam, while he read its contents. He hesitated. "It seems," he said at last, "that your laundry has been found. It is in this room. Our position has been entirely justified. Your shirts are washed and ironed, but they have been detained here for reprocessing, because by inadvertence the starch was omitted. You will have them tomorrow, starched."

The day was won. Without knowing it, he had played directly into my hands, but years of experience in dealing with success now warned me that this was the time for magnanimity, not crowing. Smiling, I quoted to him Abraham Lincoln's remark, made in reference to one of his generals, that he preferred "starch in the man rather than in his shirt." It was my way of telling him that I never have my own shirts ironed with starch.

The manager shrugged. He turned, received the package of shirts from an assistant, and handed them to me. We shook hands warmly. Although the one-hundred-per-cent-successful outcome of our meeting had been largely unexpected, I was not unprepared even for this eventuality. Still holding his hand, I clapped him on the shoulder and said, "Isn't it fine that two men, each trained to a peak of creative usefulness by our great system of economic and personal incentives, can meet as we have and exchange views openly and without fear, thus adding to man's centuries-long struggle for understanding and freedom?"

He nodded wordlessly, and we parted. I turned and walked toward my elevator, ignoring the confused babble of voices behind me engaged in excited interrogation, recapitulation, and speculation. I pressed the elevator button. As I stood there, it occurred to me that many American men in their middle years might be suddenly depressed to find themselves, immediately after a personal success, standing in a hotel sub-basement with a package of laundry in their arms. I knew, however, that the most dangerous part of any crisis is its aftermath, the time of letdown. This is when the human system, wearied by tension and hyperbole, is all too apt to become exhausted and to indulge itself in destructive reflection. This knowledge enabled me to put the thought aside. I watched the needle on the indicator above the elevator door. The car was moving downward, but soon, I knew, it would rise again, taking me with it.

Farewell to the
Giant Perch Society

(Afterthoughts on the Great Starch Debate)

That elevator that Mr. Nixon was waiting for at the end of the previous chapter did pick him up and, after a bumpy start, carried him all the way to the top floor—an ascent beyond the dreams of parody, and still, in retrospect, one that only the author of *Six Crises* could find entirely unhilarious. Absolute humorlessness has always been a formidable political asset in this country, and Mr. Nixon continues to prove almost every day that his is the true gift. It seems a shame, though, to watch him wasting his stuff on the Presidency, for the wholly literal mind is so rare a comedy resource that, wherever found, it should be fenced off, labelled, visited, photographed at dawn and sunset, and honored in guidebooks, like the Grand Canyon. Mr. Nixon, without ever trying, used to be funnier than Mort Sahl and Lennie Bruce put together; inside the White House, he is merely funnier than Herbert Hoover, which, at this moment in history, often doesn't seem funny at all. What we have here, in short, is another failure of conservation. The glum weight of his job is wearing Mr. Nixon's noble ponderosity down to mere foothills of cant, and before those stone escarpments and immense deadpan flats are entirely gone, we should look back and remember what we have lost. Here is Mr. Nixon in 1966, at the height of his powers, as gratefully observed by this writer in the Comment page of *The New Yorker:*

Custom and continuity are so lacking in these quick times that it was downright heartwarming to hear Richard M. Nixon warning us once again about the creepy, infinitely devious ways of the Communist Party. Prolonged absence from the national fireside has not diminished Mr. Nixon's fondness for an old-fashioned, heavily plotted mystery, and the other day when he took down his old Red Story Book, opened it to a new chapter, turned the lights low, and began to read aloud in that deep, chilling voice, we instantly threw ourself down in front of the hearth in our old listening position, belly to the floor and chin cupped in hands, and scanned the embers for devil faces and F.B.I. men. This tale had opened familiarly enough—with the Attorney General, a few days earlier, identifying a national youth group as a Communist-front organization. Perhaps *too* familiarly. At a time when the Communist Party seems incapable of commanding more than the minutest loyalty or interest among the young, we would have guessed that this creaky old plot device would arouse only disbelief in the national audience —but we would have been wrong. The organization, the W. E. B. DuBois Clubs of America, was at once violently attacked and stoutly defended. Members of a Brooklyn branch were beaten by a mob, and the club headquarters in San Francisco were destroyed by an explosion.

It was at this unhappy point that Mr. Nixon's reading actually began, and gratefully, almost magically, we felt ourself slipping away from the troubled, hard-edged world and off on the wings of adventure. The true, sinister nature of the DuBois Clubs is to be found, we were told, not so much in their program as in their title. The group is named for the late Negro sociologist Dr. W. E. B. Dubois, and that name is pronounced as he pronounced it—"Duboys"— rather than the more Gallic "Dubwa." Indeed, if the name is said in a careless, everyday, Commie-rat manner, it sounds almost exactly like "the Boys' Club of America," the name of a worthy recreation-and-guidance organization for boys, whose national chairman is none other than—Richard M. Nixon! Suddenly we felt the hairs rise on the back of our neck, and we whispered, "Great Scott! You mean . . ." Yes, he *did* mean. Since the Attorney General's declaration, the Boys' Club of America has received a number of threatening letters and telephone calls from super-patriots, and its executives now fear a drop in donations. The DuBois Clubs, Mr. Nixon said, "are not unaware of the confusion they are causing among our supporters and among many other good citizens." This, he said, is "an almost classic example of Communist deception and duplicity."

The more we reflect on Mr. Nixon's chiller, the more exciting and threatening it grows. Not since SMERSH, it seems, has there been an organization with so demoralizing a monicker and so devastating a program. Even the briefest reflection makes it clear that the founders of the DuBois Clubs of America must have plotted against the Boys' Club from the very beginning, and thus must have *wanted* the Attorney General to call them Communist! How cunningly they counted on the American habits of blurry diction and slipshod listening! What defense can there be against attacks on other precious national institutions by this foul technique of assonance and conquest? Think of the awful consequences when the Attorney General is forced to announce that the New York Stork Exchange (ostensibly an innocent band of ornithologists) is a Communist-front organization! The possibilities are so diverse and frightening that lately we have almost been able to hear the sound of muffled laughter rising from a manhole on our street, where the sneaky Reds are meeting in a sewer to draw up the bylaws for the Mary Conn Legion and for that celebrated anglers' club, the Giant Perch Society. We don't want to scare Mr. Nixon, but the last name to come echoing out of that sewer seems a particularly dangerous one, since it sounds like a group formed only to celebrate some nice old grandmother's birthday. It's called the Gran Holt Party.

Mr. Nixon, of course, paid no attention to the laughter coming out of that manhole, and thus became President. Politics, one keeps discovering, is not a joking matter, and an editorialist is constantly forced into the realization that candidates and statesmen in this country can achieve instant success simply

by pursuing with the utmost seriousness what he has first proposed in jest. Observe, for example, the satiric Christmas-book
list on page 144, where there is mention of a "12-inch stereo
recording of Senator Dirksen's annual reading of 'A Visit from
St. Nicholas' to the Senate pageboys." Less than a year after this
fanciful mild surmise first saw print, the late Illinois honey-
dripper made his debut as a recording artist, eventually cutting
a biscuit called "Gallant Men" that quickly jumped to the
top of the charts and launched him up into orbit beside
Connie Francis and the Beach Boys.

At about the same time, in another piece of misplaced
jocularity intended to mock the political careers of such new
Disraelis as George Murphy and Bud Wilkinson, I announced
the Presidential candidacy of "novelist and critic Manly Taylor,"
who declared himself (in part), like this:

> "One has considered as always the other fighters in the
> ring, having seen them at achingly close range from the
> lonely if somewhat existential vantage point of a two-hun-
> dred-dollar front-row seat inside one's head, and one has felt
> only the rising bile of an honest American contempt in
> one's craw at the sight of such a tawdry band of soft scufflers
> and unwilling mixers—this blue-chinned cutie, now gone
> limp in the belly, who once went the full fifteen for the
> Big One and came, one still cannot believe it, within a
> whisker of getting the duke but who, by the wheezing looks
> of him in early rounds now, has lost even the muscle to put
> over during the clinches his old jab-jabbing rabbity blows
> behind the ears and over the kidneys; that plainsman with
> the fake good looks of straight, unpunched jaw and un-
> bloodied nose, a good enough boy, one does not doubt, in
> his own back yard but who so wistfully lacks the necessary
> slum-taught ring savvy and the knowing, empty-bellied rage
> that comes only from a hundred back-alley scraps with the
> Eastern political and literary *mafiosi*; and all the others, the
> Golden Boys gone scared and the fattened flyweights with
> the scar tissue now Piltdown-thick on their eyebrows—and
> one, however unwillingly at last, sees the need to leave

one's seat; to stand up and peel down, revealing the old, much used but entirely serviceable biceps and deltoids, still hardened and knotted after all those sad cocktail-party Donnybrooks; and to borrow a pair of eight-ounce Everlasts and a dependable cup, for they will not take away rounds for low, groin-paralyzing blows in this particular fight; and to step up there, through the ropes and under the glaring American lights, and hear the roars again and feel the good fear and the dexedrine of hope.

"The act of political commitment is never casual. It is reminiscent, magical and dendroid, and therefore potentially unexistential and semi-totalitarian, but offering a preorgasmic tension and membership in the Resistance to the American cancer. . . . One has considered one's qualifications. One is very good, very good indeed, on television, though one is ashamed to admit it, recognizing such talent as possibly constituting a wound to the psyche administered in an old firefight against the most dangerous platoons of our culture. One remembers one's participation in a certain television panel during which a senator, a literate enough member of the species, stated his opinion that Dickens, Bill Faulkner, and Hank James were the best writers he had read; and one recalls one's surprised hurt, so like the wound of a woman's refusal, at the calculated omission of oneself. What had one ever done, one wondered, to cause him to drop that sneaky bomb?

"Yes, one will Go In. And while one is still counting up one's assets, one might as well put down the coolest card of all—one's lack of a platform. One will extemporize it, building it out of one's own store of dialectical lumber and hand-forged anagrammatical tenpenny nails, never knowing week by week, right down to the first Tuesday in November, what the structure will look like in the end, or what kind of shadow its minarets and cupolas will cast across the filthy, tranquillized desert of the American Political Unconscious. One accepts the challenge."

"Manly Taylor" fared badly in the early Presidential polls and withdrew, but last year, dropping the pseudonym but often employing the gutsy-elevated style of stump rhetoric I had predicted for him, he actually ran for Mayor of New York in the Democratic primary. His campaign was entertaining and therefore doomed, but even so, he won enough votes away from other liberal candidates to insure the nomination of Mario Procaccino. In the autumn, when it looked very much as if Mr. Procaccino, in turn, would unseat Mayor John V. Lindsay, I made secret preparations to leave town, for it was clear to me (if to nobody else) that the whole thing was my fault. Luckily, Mr. Procaccino conducted a campaign that easily surpassed satire—a campaign inconceivable even to a Voltaire—and Lindsay squeaked in.

I cannot conclude these Baruchian memoirs without mention of the one candidate to damage my reputation as a king-maker. I proposed him for senator at the same time I was putting forward Manly Taylor, but nothing happened. The trial balloon ascended prettily, but my man simply ignored it. It seems a pity. This Nestor is retired now and perhaps thinks of himself as being too old to achieve much clout on the major senatorial committees, but I would vote for him tomorrow if he would let me. The voice, I still believe, deserves marble:

Kumquat, Fla.—Spud Clancy, the colorful baseball manager, today announced that he is a candidate for senator in his home state. Addressing a surprised group of baseball writers in the dugout just after his club had completed its fifth day of spring training here, the grizzled veteran of the baseball wars tossed his peaked cap into the political ring in the course of a typically pungent non-stop monologue that sometimes left his listeners far behind.

"Now, I tell you," he stated at one point, "I read somewhere that feller out West, out in Tulsa or somewhere, that feller who's almost in the same line of work as I am and he coaches that sport where the players is all so big they look like eleven Kluszewskis or eleven Frank Howards out there, he turned in his whistle and says he's gonna go to Washington maybe and be a United States senator, and his you might say supporters and fans there announce it's because he is so good at buildin' character out there all these years with his boys that now he's gonna build character in Washington. Well, that got me to thinkin', and I see right away that he has been buildin' character for maybe fifteen years in a sport in which there is maybe ten games they play every year and that makes one hundred and fifty games of buildin' character for him, which is twelve full games less of character buildin' than I do in even one season, not counting the World Series, which I'm not in so much now any more, but I been managing and coaching twenty years so I'm more up on character buildin' than he is and then some. And maybe my character buildin' is even harder than his because not all my players come from where they get to join those Greek clubs and play mandolins and run around all year with them coeds and some of them can't even hit behind the runner they got so little character and I have to start them on character from you might say scratch. So with all this experience I got, I decided I'm going up to Washington, too, if they send me, and build a little character on my own."

The Old Wizard then went on to expatiate on Washington and his views of the political life. "I uster know Washington when I was in the other league," he said, "and the fans they got there have a club that's been down in the cellar so long they don't remember what the players look like or what they do for a livin' and they even suspicion maybe the players is mushroom growers or snapshot developers they're down in the cellar so much. And you might say it's just the same with the Senate, which has players that aren't puttin' out but are layin' back and readin' newspapers all the time and only gettin' up to get a drink of water out of the cooler, and as a club the Senate hasn't been hittin' much better than like .195 since the days when Henry Clay was batting leadoff and they was somethin' to see.

"Also, you have to remember I've seen these politicians every year, which is when some of them come out to the ballpark on Opening Day and throw out that honorary first ball to start the season for the photographers, and for goodness sake the way they throw the ball is like your Aunt Hattie throwin' a ball of knitting to the family cat, and I figure that already I know more about being a senator than they know about being a ballplayer if that's the best they can throw. Because what a senator has to make mostly is decisions, and what else do I have to make all day but decisions, such as hit or run and such as whether I should go out there and take the ball away from my pitcher who has just thrown two pitches all the way to the screen and might bean the owner in his box with the next pitch, or leave him in there because the other feller I got waiting in the bullpen has got the other trouble, which is his control is so good his pitches keep hitting the outfield fences all the time on the fly because he hits the other fellers' bats with them? And that's a harder decision than what the senators have to make, which is mostly whether to spend more money out of Fort Knox to build a new bridge over a creek back home so the voters won't get their feet wet on Election Day when they go to town to vote for that senator who remembered how they like to vote without mud all over their feet.''

Sad Arthur

(Go Hesse, Young Man)

One morning, Sad Arthur, the banker's son, rose and garbed himself. Softly and lovingly the bedroom Mazdas bathed him as, supple-limbed, he drew on the new costume of his decision. Over his baggy BVD gaiters Sad Arthur put on his resplendent Belstaff Riding Suit with its storm-proof pockets, storm-cuff sleeves, heavy-duty zipper, snapdown pockets, and buckled mandarin-style collar. Sad Arthur bent and stepped into his Beau Geste Rough Rider boots with full-zippered backs, adjustable heel and instep straps, and imbedded front-and-back steel friction plates. Sad Arthur pulled on his Leathertogs genuine-leather jacket with transverse zipper and heavy-duty wrist snaps, and strapped on his stud wristbands and seven-inch stud belt. Delicately Sad Arthur balanced his yellow Foster Grants above his lofty brow and then picked up his flocked fuchsia Fury Helmet. Sad Arthur's mirror, which loved him unquenchably, watched in sad surprise as Sad Arthur left the bedroom forever. Then the mirror fell into a reflective mood, wondering once again how it had ever lost Altman's.

Sad Arthur entered the veranda and stood behind the chair where his father, the banker, was catching a few z's. The good banker, who that week had taken a bath in Leasco, was having a troubled dream about unholy ablutions. In time, he awoke, aware of the presence of leather. "Is that you, Sad Arthur?" he said.

Sad Arthur remained silent, his arms folded. Long ago, he had learned the lesson of the closed yap, the magic of the monosyllable. In the sullen, downward-hanging head, the lidded eye, the unheeding ear, there lay invulnerable peace. There was strange power in this youthful demeanor that willed nothing. Faced with it, the others—the teachers and talkers—became irritated, then flustered, then enraged, then placating, then suppliant. Like a flock of bees, they gave up their golden treasure to him who merely seemed to doze by the hive. So Sad Arthur stood unmoving. Sunbeams meditated in the unshorn locks on his neck.

"What is it already?" the banker demanded. "Come around here where I can see you." He sighed. "No—on second thought, don't."

"You know what is in my mind," Sad Arthur said at last. "I would leave home and join the Holy Terrors. Like."

"I don't get it," confessed the good banker. "My son the bike freak."

"With the Holy Terrors I will make Vegas," Sad Arthur said. "I wish to attain Nevada."

The banker fell silent. In his secret heart he, too, had seen himself joyful at Vegas, strolling The Sands. Several hours passed in silence, like skipped pages in a meaty volume. In time, the banker gave a start, opened his eyes, yawned, and rose from his chair. "Let me know if you attain Nevada," he said to his son. "Call us collect." He could deny nothing to this young man. Like the Mazdas and the mirror and the sunbeams, like everything and everybody, he loved Sad Arthur, though often it was hard to know why.

Sad Arthur left his home. Near the garage, his faithful companion Irving was waiting with the bikes.

"You have come," Irving said.

"I have come," said Sad Arthur, smiling.

"He was faked out," Irving said.

"He was faked out," said Sad Arthur.

"We can split," Irving said.

"We can split," said Sad Arthur.

They split.

Wandering westward, Sad Arthur and Irving found the Holy Terrors in a blighted grove near Leonia, N.J. They recognized the leader of the band, the fabled Guttheimer, and drew near. This good buddy was known for his teachings and his freaky vines. His ancient bombardier's jacket was encrusted with many a graffitic virtu and many a mottoed malediction, now all faded by wind and dust, that depicted the pain and suffering of the pilgrim's way. The Illustrated One, at ease astride his ancient Harley two-stroke banger, listened to Sad Arthur's and Irving's joyful plea to get their heads together as novitiates in the Holy Terrors, heard their deep desire to attain Nevada. He subjected them to certain rites and then, well pleased, grunted the wished-for grant. Sad Arthur and Irving were Holy Terrors at last!

Happy among brothers, boot to boot with these heavy-footed disciples and their Old Ladies, Sad Arthur wandered westward (and sometimes eastward and ditchward) on the ancient paths of Jersey. Together, the Holy Terrors bombed Bogota, deafened Dumont, horrified Hoboken, outraged Oradell, paralyzed Palisades Park, piqued Parsippany, ravaged Rahway, and were busted in Boonton. Here, within a rustic slammer, Sad Arthur drew near Guttheimer and spoke what was in his mind.

Sad Arthur said: "Hear me, O Illustrated One, for I am, you know, like troubled. I have heard your teachings and learned much. You show the world unbroken, like a well-lubed chain. From you I have learned the Eightfold Path to hop a Honda 90cc SL to a sassy quarter in thirteen with a stroker kit, trochoid pump, overboring, and velocity stacks. From you I have learned the Fivefold Path to dirty up a square Moto Guzzi 750cc Ambassador by means of laid-on chromed riser bars, extended forks, sissy bar, and STP decals. From you I have learned the Fourteenfold Path to cowboy-roll a joint while drafting on a downhill Greyhound at eighty per. All this have I learned, O Good Buddy, yet what do I see? I see this band still mucking about here in upper Jersey, no nearer Vegas than the day I fell in. So what are teachings, what is knowledge, what are dead eardrums and dropped kidneys if they do not take me to Nevada? Are you not, then, the same as my father the good banker, a mere workahubby?"

The Illustrated One's eyes were lowered, his furred mouth set in an unfathomable half-smile of understanding. He was stoned. "You are some punkins, O Sad Arthur," he said. "You are a real smart-ass. I would enlighten you with still another lesson, the Onefold Path to a bust in the mouth, only right now I gotta crash."

The next morning, Sad Arthur took his leave of the pokey. He bade farewell to the Holy Terrors. He bade farewell to the faithful Irving, who was crying. Alone, he wandered westward on his Kawasaki Three. He saw many things. He saw a small boy at a Carvel stand who had dripped chocolate ripple all over his mother's handbag. He saw a man in madras Bermudas who had just been bilked by a used-lawnmower salesman. He saw a young opossum that had just been mashed by a teen-ager in a magenta Corvette. He saw a drunken housewife weeping in front of her Sylvania color console. He saw an elderly pastor playing miniature golf in a black hairpiece. He saw a Fruehauf twelve-wheel rig lying on its side, with its cargo of disposable diapers scattered across the highway. The world was beautiful when seen this way—alone and without questions or meaning. It was beautiful to go through the world like this in childlike cool. The Illustrated One was right, Sad Arthur thought. Sad Arthur, you are some punkins.

In a sun-dappled launderette in Nutley, N.J., but a short distance from the holy ruins of the Nutley Velodrome, Sad Arthur encountered the fair Lambie, whose lips were like unto a melting Tootsie Roll. At one sight of her, he plugged in his Fender and, without thought or further ado, sang this song:

> "For love of the fair Lambie,
> The pilgrim Sad Arthur,
> Sad Arthur the erstwhile Terror,
> The fabled rubber-layer,
> Would forget Nevada
> And stay
> Here in Nutley Enn Jayyy!"

"O Sad Arthur, how marvie!" cried the entranced Lambie.

"Yes," said Sad Arthur without unbecoming modesty. "Please note the rhyme."

"O Sad Arthur, c'mere." She drew him to her, placing one heel on his instep and one hand on his ear in the position of love that is known as "Opening the Deck Chair." Then she kissed him with her lips that were like unto a melting Tootsie Roll.

Thus it was that Sad Arthur put away his boots and helmet, put away Nevada, put away his dreams and his Kawasaki to stay in Nutley and groove with the fair Lambie. He cut his hair and went to work for Lambie's father, a merchant, the owner of the Nutley Kwik Kleen Dry Cleaners. He went among the people and took on the people's ways. With Lambie, he bought six-packs and electric back-yard rotisseries, he wore His-'n-Hers flowered at-home jams, he joined the Thursday Evening Swingin' Couples League at Nutley Bowlorama. Lambie's father was pleased with him and said, "You have learned much from me, Sad Arthur."

"No," said Sad Arthur. "All that I have learned I have taught myself. I have learned to deliver a suit on Friday that was promised for Wednesday. I have learned to deliver size forty-two pants to the size thirty-four next door. I have learned to mislay ladies' dress belts, to anneal zippers, and to loosen buttons so that they will pop off upon being buttoned. I have learned to starch alpaca sweaters and imprint indelible rust stains on dress evening shirts. Most of all, I have learned the imperious Brahmin's manner that elicits abject thanks and excessive tips. Thus do I add injury and interest to the lives of these sad schnooks. It is you, rather, who have learned from me."

Lambie's father looked on Sad Arthur with admiration and surprise. "The mouth, O Sad Arthur," he said. "That mouth will get bust wide open one of these days."

Sad Arthur saw that it was time for him to resume his questing. The merchant's message, so like the parting words of Guttheimer, told him that he had come full circle. He had learned the people's ways, their business and their pleasures, and now his soul was sickened, as the soul of one who has played thrice at tick-tack-toe. He went to the fair Lambie and imparted unto her what he had decided.

"O no, Sad Arthur!" cried the fair Lambie. She placed her elbow in his abdomen and her knee against his back, in the position that is known as "Putting Away the Ironing Board," but he pushed her rudely aside.

"Tough darts, Lambie," Sad Arthur said. "It's Nevada for me. Bye now."

Why did her lips, curved in sorrow, remind him of a Cat's Paw heel?

Sad Arthur turned westward once more. On foot now, he wandered with thumb lifted, riding with any who heeded his disdainful summons. Riding silent in high cab beside some trusting trucker, Sad Arthur smiled and commended himself for having put aside still more knowledge, more habits, more mere humans. Within his stomach he felt the tiny gerbil of his Self stirring once again, heard it remount its squeaky little wheel.

Closer to Vegas at last, Sad Arthur alighted on the north bank of the great Pennsylvania Pike, and here took employment as night pumper in a modest Amoco station. Wearing the plain blue coveralls and friendly smile of his humble calling, he dispensed the golden fluid, wiped clean the insect-speckled windshield, kept track of the ladies'-room key with its giant tag. At night, between customers, he tilted back in his chair and listened to the highway. He knew he should resume his journey, should seek Nevada, yet it seemed to him that this highway had something to tell him. He felt a deep love for these broad humming lanes with their upping and downing, their easting and westing, their freight of fumes and destinations, and he sat and stayed and listened.

Years passed, and so it was at last that an ochre Caddy stopped at Sad Arthur's modest Amoco station and yielded up a bald old gent with low back pains and a large cigar. Sad Arthur looked on him and smiled.

"Sad Arthur!" cried the old gent. "Is that you? Are you here, only here? And all this time I imagined you at Nevada!"

"Yes," said Sad Arthur. "It is I, my old friend. Only I."

"What a gas!" cried the faithful Irving (for it was he), and then he laughed at his own foolish wit. "So neither of us made it to Vegas, eh? What a pair of losers!"

"Listen, my friend," said Sad Arthur, and he took Irving by the arm and led him closer to the highway's edge. "Listen to me, for I have learned the secret. The highway has taught me all. At one end of this highway, back beyond its beginning, is my father, the good banker. There too are the Illustrated One, the fair Lambie, the overturned diaper truck, my rusted old Kawasaki, and the lost size forty-two pants. At the other, beyond its ending and yet part of it as well, lies Nevada. At the same time, right now, they are all part of this highway, all one. This highway is everywhere at the same moment—the toll-taker and the toll-payer, the patient concrete and the headlong tire, the descendant swallow-dropping and the approaching open convertible, the totalled Pontiac and the greedy wrecker, the full box of Goobers on the dashboard and the emptied box of Goobers in the weeds by the roadside. This highway is the beginning and the ending, the cool and the uncool, learning and forgetting, the book revered and the book flung halfway across the room. There is no truth, no knowing, no wisdom, no Nevada, no nothing except, uh—well, simultanuity, like. So relax."

"Gosh, Sad Arthur," said Irving, "I never thought of it that way." He looked at his watch. "Well, Artie," he said hastily, "this has been real. Any time you're near Hasbrouck Heights—"

But again Sad Arthur drew him closer to the highway's edge. "Listen, faithful Irving," Sad Arthur said. "Listen to the highway. What does it say to you?"

"Well," said Irving after a while, "it sort of says 'Zoom!' "

"Yes," said Sad Arthur. He lifted his head in wonder. "Zoom!" he repeated. "Zoom-*zoom!*"

L'Après-Midi d'un Fan

(Sample TV Fare for an Autumn Sabbath)

ANNOUNCER (*blazered, crew-cut, earphoned*): Good afternoon,
sports fans, and welcome to another thrilling presentation of the
"Sunday Sports Shebang"! I'm Spike Ammidown, your host
at this roundup of great sportsmanship, great athletes, and
stirring highlights of sports events from around this great
globe of ours! Here in the next five hours, you're gonna see,
all live, and on tape, too, the ecstasy of victory and the concomitant heartache of defeat, in great climactic scenes of a
full dozen major athletic events from the four corners of the
earth, brought into your living room by our expert reporters
and camera teams, whom you can be sure are standing by at
this very minute! Right now, I'm standing here, *live*, on the
eighteenth fairway of the Pawtucket Drive-In Golf-A-Way, where
you will see this afternoon the final holes of the great $250,000
Eastern Open Miniature Golf Championship. We'll be bringing
those dramatic holes your way in just a few moments, but
right now I have a signal from Red Glebman, who is waiting
in a front-row seat in our broadcasting booth at Busch Memorial
Stadium, in St. Louis, to bring you thrilling action from the
final game of the World Series. So come in, Red!

RED GLEBMAN: Thanks, Spike, and good afternoon, ball fans!
Here, brought to you *live* from the home of the battlin' Cardi-
nals, we're in the top of the seventh inning of the seventh
and final game of the great Fall Classic. The score here is tied
up at 0–0 in a real nail-biter, and as you can see in this
special shot from our Goodyear blimp high above the Big
Muddy, the Tigers have two men on the old basepaths! As

83

the faithful Redbird fans here have learned, these Bengals from the Motor City don't know the meaning of the word "quit." Two out! Two on! Sluggin' Jim Northrup stands in. Bob Gibson, the Redbirds' ace fireballer, has gone all the way, but right now he looks mighty bushed out there. Just *listen* to this crowd! Now he's got the sign. He's taking his stretch! The runners lead away—

SPIKE AMMIDOWN (*back at the Golf-A-Way*): Thanks, Red. And thanks for that magnificent moment from the great world of the national pastime. We'll be getting back to you real soon. Meantime, I have word that Jim Croddy is standing by at the finals of the World Championship Garage Attendants' Parking Rodeo, out in Los Angeles, where he'll be bringing you all that thrilling action *live*, so come on in, Jim!

JIM CRODDY: Thanks a million, Spike, and good afternoon, parking fans! I'm here at the foot of the lower-ramp straightaway of the Acme Minute-Park Garage, in the heart of downtown L.A., where today we'll see the final events of this thrilling Parking Rodeo including the $50,000 Top-Floor-to-Street-Level Compact Car Delivery Sprints, in which the nine finalists, from a Le Mans start, will vie for control of this single steep ramp! Here beside me, *live*, at this moment, is Luther (Ace) Purdy, the defending champion in this event, who is currently in third place in the over-all standings with 12,564,811.49 points. Ace, you dropped back to third yesterday when the judges gave you only 24.41 points on Style at the conclusion of your great run in the Unlimited Class Curved-Ramp Backup. How do you feel about that?

ACE PURDY: Well, Jim, I'm glad you ast me that, because I sure got a raw deal. I mean, I don't want to fault these great judges or nothin', but when that fender fell offn the Jag at the top of the ramp, I didn't have nothin' to do with it a-tall. I mean, when I jumped into that Jag I seen that that fender was just held on there with a little piece of old baling wire or something. One of these crazy rookies musta whanged it off in one of the qualifyin' runs. I'm appealing those Style points to the International Federation. Just see if I don't!

JIM CRODDY: Good for you, Ace! And thanks for those fighting sentiments from a great sporting gentleman!

SPIKE AMMIDOWN (*breaking in again*): Thanks, Jim, for that exciting on-the-spot interview. We have an urgent signal from Red Glebman at Busch Memorial Stadium, which means that things must be popping at that final Series game! We'll get back to Red in just a minute, at the conclusion of this important message from our sponsor.

SPIKE AMMIDOWN: Well, here we are again, fans, with more of your "Sunday Sports Shebang"! Before we get back to Red Glebman, who seems to have some mighty hot news for us—take it easy there, Red, boy!—we want to jump down to Tex Guttweiler, who is standing by, *live*, at the finals of the Panhandle Senior Mixed Doubles Tennis Championships, at the Broomstraw Country Club, in Amarillo. It's all yours, Tex!

TEX GUTTWEILER (*whispering*): Thanks, Spike, and good afternoon, mixed-doubles fans! This *has* to be great timing, because at this moment the finals stand here at match point! Mrs. Eloise MacKittrup and her partner, Bob Spurge, are trailing Mr. and Mrs. Billy-Joe Jenkins, 1–6, 0–5, in this second set. It's love–40 and Mrs. MacKittrup is serving. Right now, things look mighty black for the MacKittrup-Spurge duo, but as everyone down here in the Panhandle knows, they're all heart, and I wouldn't be surprised if we were about to see the beginning of a great fighting comeback. Mrs. MacKittrup is gritting her teeth. She toes the line—here's the serve! Oop—she hit it into the net! It's a fault. Here's the old second serve. Uh-oh—it's *out*! It's a good eight feet out, and this match is over! And there you have it, folks, *live* from Amarillo—the Double Fault of the Week! Back to you, Spike, fella.

SPIKE AMMIDOWN: How 'bout that, Tex! Thanks for that great on-the-spot coverage. Now, before we go to Red Glebman at the World Series—relax, Red, for crying out loud! It's just a game—we want to bring you a fascinating feature story that I taped in person last week at the village of Izquirra, high in the Basque country of northern Spain, as an exclusive for the

"Sunday Sports Shebang." So, without more ado, we'll roll that for you. Over to me, in Izquirra! . . . Good afternoon, folks! It's I, Spike Ammidown, here in the main street of Izquirra, a mighty long way from Pawtucket, from where I'll be showing you this from next Sunday. Such is the wonder of our shrinking, sports-loving globe! Today I'm going to bring you, exclusive and for the first time on any network, the annual championship game of Qub, the national Basque sport that is played only here in Izquirra. As you can see, I am surrounded by the villagers, who are garbing themselves with their interesting equipment and planning team strategy just before the whistle that will start this exciting eight-hour contest. Standing beside me is Raimondo Uzcuden, the Mayor of Izquirra and the only inhabitant who speaks English, who will explain to us some of the fine points of Qub. Tell us, Mayor Uzcuden, how many players are there on a side in Qub?

MAYOR UZCUDEN: Eet depends.

SPIKE AMMIDOWN: I see. And these tall wicker baskets the players are strapping to their heads—what are they called?

MAYOR UZCUDEN: Zhey have no name. Just old baskets.

SPIKE AMMIDOWN: Yes. Now, as I understand it, the players *catch* the ball, or *qub*, in these head-baskets and then dribble or pass the *qub* to their teammates at top speed. And the players must keep their hands in their pockets *at all times*. Is that correct?

MAYOR UZCUDEN: Ees correct.

SPIKE AMMIDOWN: And what is the ball, or *qub*, made of?

MAYOR UZCUDEN: Sometimes ees a stone. Sometimes ees ball of feathers. This year, ees a Coke bottle.

SPIKE AMMIDOWN: Golly! And how are the two goals demarcated?

MAYOR UZCUDEN: Uphill goal ees Don Federico's donkey. Downhill goal ees *bodega* window. Goalie pays eef window gets broken. Keeps heem on toes, no?

SPIKE AMMIDOWN: Thank you, Mayor! *Gracias, amigo!* And there you have it, Qub fans—the ancient rules of this ancient game! We'll be back a little later with some great action scenes of this dangerous and lightning-fast sport, but first here's another message from our sponsor.

SPIKE AMMIDOWN: Here we are, sports lovers, back in the good old U.S.A. and *live* at the Pawtucket Golf-A-Way, all ready with more of your "Sunday Sports Shebang." A few moments ago, we brought you a taped view of some of the complexities of that dangerous Basque game of Qub. Now we know you're ready for simpler, more familiar fare—a game that you all know and love. In short, it's pro football time! Buddy Pitts and his crew are perched high above the fifty-yard line at Memorial Stadium in Ottumwa, Iowa, where the second quarter of the game between the Ottumwa Chiefs and the Hannibal Elephants is in progress. Right after this live report, we'll get back to Red Glebman and the World Series in St. Louis. So take it, Buddy Pitts!

BUDDY PITTS: Thanks, Spike, and good afternoon, grid fans! Here in Ottumwa, the score is tied, 24–24, midway through the second quarter in this rock-'em, sock-'em game between the hard-nosed behemoths of the Des Moines Valley League. There's time out on the field, so I'm gonna ask Pudge Spivack, the great former All-League guard who is our play-spotter to come in and analyze that last play for you. Pudge?

PUDGE SPIVACK: Thanks, Buddy. Now, as most of you fans must have recognized, that last play was the Two-X Blue-29 Sprint-out Deep Option. As you can see on the blackboard here, Whitey Bamberger takes the snap, fakes to a running back coming across, fakes to the fullback cutting inside, and then rolls out to his right behind the two pulling guards. The center, Sprazzuolo, has to trap the strongside tackle, O'Toole, and the *offensive* strongside tackle, Rudinsky, double-teams the middle linebacker, "Big Mother" Majurciewicz, with Spranghausen, the leading guard. Meantime, the tight end, Krock, takes off with the snap, fakes a right turn-in, then fakes a left zig-out, and *then* runs a straight fly pattern. The wide receiver, Poole, fakes a buttonhook, then actually *does* buttonhook and floats back to take a safety-valve pass if needed. The split end, "Fingers" Guildenschaft, meantime fakes a five-yard loop-out to the right, then cuts back for a little look-in pass over center. On *dee*-fense, the Elephants' corner linebacker, Karakashian, keyed on Krock—unless, of course, Guildenschift had overshafted, it which case Karakashian's key on Krock collapses the corner covered by Holtzapple, the safety man, who was in tight on the Shirley Red Dog. Of course, on this play Whitey Bamberger dropped the snap from center and had to fall on the ball, so none of this made much difference. O.K., Buddy?

BUDDY PITTS: O.K., Pudge, and thanks. I'm sure all our millions of viewers were glad to have their analysis of that last play clearly confirmed by you. We'll have more football action in just a few minutes, but meantime it's back to Spike Ammidown in Pawtucket. Take it, Coach!

SPIKE AMMIDOWN: Thank you, thank you, Buddy. There's nothing like football for thrills, is there, fans? Well, it's all over at Busch Memorial Stadium, folks. The final game of the 1968 Series is history! Red Glebman is standing by with a recap wrapup of that great chapter of the Fall Classic, but since the game is over, we can wait and hear from Red in just a few minutes. Meantime, here at the Pawtucket Golf-A-Way, I see that the final-round leaders in this $250,000 Eastern Miniature Golf Open are now on the fifteenth tee, so I think I'd better make you all familiar with the layout of this challenging final eighteenth hole. As you can see, this *has* to be a magnificent test, measuring sixty-five feet four inches—one of those truly demanding par 3s. So far in the tourney, there have only been four aces carded here, each entitling the lucky player to another round at no extra charge. From this elevated tee, a long hitter can aim across this narrow, tilted teeter-totter, hoping to drop the ball safely on the other side, beyond the Enchanted Forest, and then straight into the Gnome's open mouth—a shot that will come out the pipe on the other side of Toad Hall and right onto the old green. *Or,* if he's a little weak off the tee, he can play it safe by fading his drive up this little garden path, between the rows of cockleshells, past the rotating vanes of Little Bopeep's windmill—which takes cool, cool timing, believe you me—and then over London Bridge and onto the green. Even if his shot fades too much, which is possible today in this left-to-right wind, and goes off the bridge, there's just a *chance* that the ball will hit one of these little concrete lily pads and—

But now I see it's time for our stations to identify themselves, so I'll let them come in now and, uh, identify themselves from coast to coast. Now, don't forget to stay right with us, sports fans, because we have plenty more action to bring your way this afternoon. We'll have further *live* coverage from all those great events you've already seen, including good old Red Glebman's on-the-spot summary of that big seventh game of the World Series. And, above and beyond all this, we'll bring you a special report, relayed to you *live* by Pacific Telstar, on the Two Million Metre Himalayan Walkathon, straight from Darjeeling; the Prep School Touch Football Play of the Week, taped at yesterday's Donnybrook between the Seniors and Upper Middlers at Governor Dummer; water-skiing grandmothers at Lake Tahoe; and lots, *lots* more! So don't go 'way, sports fans. Stay right there in your seats and get ready for more healthful, thrilling moments on your "Sunday Sports Shebang"!

Keeping Up
with the Outs

Club's Début Separates the Ins from the Outs

It wasn't easy to find an Arthur at Arthur Wednesday night, but everyone else was there—Caterine and D.D. and Jane, Jake and Mike and Rudolf, all those "in" people who know that Arthur is a place and not a person.—Angela Taylor in *The New York Times*.

One of the people who didn't know that Arthur is a place and not a person is Mrs. Herbert W. Spangenberg of 221-11 Twenty-sixth Avenue, Bayside, who almost missed the news altogether. As it was, she caught up with the fact that Arthur is the name of Sybil Burton's new discothèque three days late, and, as she said later, it was the funniest thing that she noticed it at all. She was out in the hall late Sunday night just flopping down this big bunch of newspapers on top of the two trash baskets and the garbage pail and the three full wastebaskets—it's *something* the way the papers and trash pile up at the Spangenbergs' over the weekend, especially if they have friends in for supper on Friday or Saturday night, or if young Herbert, Jr. (who is known as Hub), is home on pass from Fort Belvoir—when her eye was caught by this flash of a headline that began with the name "Arthur." Well, as she told Mr. Spangenberg a few minutes later, and as she explained more fully the next morning in a telephone call to her friend Janet Mulleavy (Mrs. Francis T. Mulleavy, of 31-09 Two Hundred and Fourteenth Place), she had just been trying to flump the newspapers into any sort of a pile that wouldn't fall off the trash cans and onto the floor and make Angelo, the super, sore in the morning, and she had been holding the apartment door open with one foot and trying at the same time to keep Bingo, the Spangenbergs' Boston bull, from coming out into the hall; but after that glimpse of the word "Arthur" she pressed the little button on the door that releases the lock, and then closed the door, thus confining Bingo, and then went back and riffled through all the papers right there in the hall until she found the story in the old Friday *Times* with the headline, "ARTHUR, ONCE A HAIRDO, IS NOW A DISCOTHÈQUE." The really funny thing about it all, as she told Herb and, later on, Janet, is that she doesn't care much one way or the other about discothèques, but she always sort of pricks up her ears when she sees the word "Arthur," and that's because "Arthur" to her means her brother, of course—Arthur Briscoe, of Canandaigua, N.Y. Not that Art Briscoe gets in the paper very often, or anything like that. He is eleven years older than Mrs. Spangenberg (she was Florence Briscoe before she went to Cornell on a Regents' scholarship in the fall of 1936; she dropped out after that one year and married Herb Spangenberg, who was a senior and a Kappa Sig), and five years ago Art retired after forty-one years with Northern Mohawk Power and Light. Florence and her brother have sort of lost touch with each other over the years, though they always exchange Christmas presents, and last year the Briscoes came to town over Washington's Birthday, staying at the Spangenbergs' for three whole days. But Florence cares about Arthur, and that's why she always looks twice when she sees an Arthur in the papers because it might be Art. Oh, not an obituary—Florence isn't gloomy that way, even though Art is in his sixties now—but you never can tell. And there was that time back in 1948 when Florence did find Arthur's name in the paper—his name *and* his picture—when he was an alternate delegate to the Republican National Convention, which was held in Philadelphia. Nobody in the New York delegation got sick or anything, so Art didn't get to vote for Governor Dewey at the convention, but Florence still has the clipping somewhere, and probably that's how she got the habit of noticing the name Arthur in the newspapers.

Florence Spangenberg read the *Times* story about the discothèque named Arthur right through while standing out in the hall in her green polka-dot cotton bathrobe, and then she tore out the story and headline, and after pushing the other button that reset the front-door lock and shushing Bingo, who had begun to bark when she came back in, she took the clipping into the bedroom and told Herb about how funny it was, her mistaking a new discothèque for her brother. Herb was in bed, almost asleep but trying to watch a Bob Hope movie called *Paris Holiday* on the Late Show, because Anita Ekberg was in it, and he listened to Florence, nodding his head to show her he was paying attention but really watching the TV screen, but when his wife began to read the clipping aloud he said, "Oh, what *is* all this, Flo, for Christ's sake, anyway?" and she stopped. But the next morning, after Herb had gone to work, she called Janet, and Janet agreed that it was really peculiar learning about the discothèque named Arthur in that funny way. Janet Mulleavy then added that she wondered how Florence could have missed knowing about Arthur for all this time, because it had been in all the columns for months and months now, and people were always talking about it on the Johnny Carson Show, because it was *the* place to go, as all the "in" people knew. "Well," Florence Spangenberg said, "I just didn't see it anywhere before last night out in the hall. I guess I must be getting old, or something, but I didn't see anything about it." Pretty soon she hung up. Her feelings were hurt.

•

A fleet of limousines and buses hauled an adequately star-studded cargo of partygoers to a Staten Island country house last night for a supper dance in an elegant pink-and-white striped tent. Trumbull Barton and John L. McHugh gave the gathering in honor of their old friend Dame Margot Fonteyn.

. . . the list also included Mrs. René Bouché, Mr. and Mrs. William Colleran (Lee Remick), Mr. and Mrs. Martin Gabel (Arlene Francis), Alan Jay Lerner and Oliver Messel, Lord Snowdon's uncle. The Livingston Biddles had declined, and Mr. Blass sent his regrets. Truman Capote, on the other hand, did not answer his invitation.—Charlotte Curtis, in *The New York Times.*

Another person who didn't turn up at the Trumbull Barton–John L. McHugh party for Dame Margot Fonteyn is Owen Sperry, thirty-nine, of 18 East Eleventh Street. If Mr. Sperry hadn't been in bed with the flu and a temperature of just over a hundred and one, he probably wouldn't have known about the party at all, because he doesn't usually get around to the society and women's pages in the *Times,* but that morning (it was a Tuesday), after he had called his secretary and told her again that he wouldn't be in and explained that the doctor had said that there was nothing to do for these things but stay in bed and take aspirin and drink lots of water and wait it out, sometimes for as long as ten days, he hung up, and then, with his head propped up on three pillows, he read his way languidly and slowly through the *Times,* occasionally falling into a light doze and then waking and going on with the paper. He found the story about the supper dance and read it all the way through—almost a column and a half—and it occurred to him that it was the first time he had ever come upon a social report that ended with a list of absentees. He tossed the *Times* on the floor, poured himself another glass of water and made himself drink it, and lay back and closed his eyes, and in his mind he composed what seemed to be a logical continuation to the story: ". . . Truman Capote, on the other hand, did not answer his invitation. Curiously, Mr. and Mrs. Owen Sperry (Adelaide Jencks) received no invitation to the party in the first place, and neither did Miss Linda Sperry, 12, the student. Reached late last night, Mr. Sperry stated that he certainly would have acknowledged the invitation, one way or the other, had it appeared in the Sperry mailbox. The list of the uninvited also included Mrs. Howard

Jencks, of Pelham, who is Miss Sperry's grandmother, Dr. Leonard Farbson, the dedicated influenza fighter, Peter D. Falkenhausen, who is Mr. Sperry's employer, and—" Here Sperry, who was undoubtedly feeling his fever, decided to go on and make a mental list of everyone he knew who could not possibly have been at the party. Luckily, he had only gone through a dozen-odd names when he got stuck trying to remember the name of the old lady who had lived with three Pomeranians on the ground floor of the Sperry's old apartment on Christopher Street (she never would have left the dogs to go way out to Staten Island for a supper dance), and the effort of thinking back and muttering "Matthews? . . . Marx? . . . Mameluke?" soon put him to sleep once again.

By afternoon, Sperry had forgotten about the Barton-McHugh party. He tried to do a little manuscript reading in bed (Mr. Sperry is an editor with a small, conservative, and not very successful publishing house), but he couldn't pay attention, and he put in a couple of hours dazedly watching quiz programs on the TV set. A little after four, Linda Sperry came home from school. She inspected him from the doorway through her horn-rimmed glasses and announced, "Boy, you look *terrible.*" Pretty soon, Mrs. Sperry came home from her job at the uptown girls' school where she teaches remedial reading, and set about neatening up the sickroom. Owen Sperry got up and shaved while his wife remade the bed with fresh sheets, and then he changed into clean pajamas and climbed back into bed. He felt a little better, and there were some branches of new lilacs in a vase on his bureau. Later, he ate a light supper of cold madrilène and aspirin. That evening, his wife read aloud to him—a couple of chapters from an old Evelyn Waugh novel—and by ten-fifteen he was asleep, with the lights out and the door closed.

For the past three or four years, however, Owen Sperry had been bothered with insomnia—not the kind that keeps you from falling asleep but the kind that nudges you awake sometime between four and six in the morning—and on this night he awoke again long before first light. He lay there in the dark, his pajama collar damp with sweat, and muzzily cursed the ineffectual sleeping pill he had taken. In recent months, Sperry's night thoughts have been of a singularly depressing nature—cancer, flash fires, automobile collisions, his lack of progress in his office, recent cruelties and stupidities of his own making—but this time something made him remember the elegant party he had read about in the *Times*. In the dark, in the middle of the night, he felt bitter about it, instead of amused, and he finally said aloud, "Well, why *weren't* we invited?" He didn't know the hosts, that was why, and after a little reflection he realized that he probably wouldn't have known one guest there, either. He didn't know any real celebrities—only a couple of moderately acclaimed authors. Once, when he was fourteen, he had played ping-pong with Fay Wray at a resort hotel in New Hampshire. He and his wife would have had a lousy time at that party; they would have been stuck with each other in a corner, trying to make conversation and pretending they didn't care. And he had just about forgotten how to dance. Oh, it wasn't himself and his wife he cared about so much; it was Linda. When he was in college, he had gone to some pretty nifty débutante parties, but he and Adelaide hadn't kept up with that sort of world after their marriage. They weren't much for parties. But now he had to face it: there was a pretty good chance that Linda would never get to go to a supper dance by limousine. His fault. He lay there and saw Linda—Linda grown up but looking the same, with her brown hair and her glasses and her plump arms—standing unnoticed outside a pink-and-white striped tent, with music coming through the night trees. Next thing he knew, he was crying.

Sperry has had enough experience with night thoughts to know that the thing to do is get out of bed, turn on the lights, find a snack—anything to break the chain. Out of habit, he now got up and fumbled for his bathrobe in the dark, even though his wife was sleeping in the study during his sickness and wouldn't have been awakened if he had just stayed there in bed and read a book for a while. He found an old quilt and wrapped it around his shoulders and then went down to the dark hall and into the living room. He flicked on the lights, picked up some magazines from the stack on the coffee table, and sat down in the wing chair, tucking the quilt around his feet. It was strange being in the living room for the first time in so long. Over by the window, his wife's house plants looked different, as if he had surprised them in the night. Then Sperry heard creaking and footsteps, and his wife came into the room. She was barefoot, wearing just her nightgown, and her arms were crossed in front of her. Her eyes were blinking in the light.

"What on *earth*?" she said. "What are you doing up? I heard you banging around."

"Couldn't sleep," Sperry explained. "You know how I get."

"But you're sick." She leaned over and felt his forehead. "Listen," she said, "as long as you're all covered up here, just sit tight and I'll take your temperature again."

She went out, and when she came back she was wearing her bathrobe and shaking down the thermometer. She stuck it in his mouth and sat on the arm of the next chair and waited. Even with the sleepy, concerned expression on her face and the hair clips over her ears, she looked pretty to him. It was something special, the two of them being in the living room in the middle of the night.

She took the thermometer back. "Only ninety-nine two," she said. "And now back to bed with you. I think you're getting better."

"I do, too," said Owen Sperry. He followed her down the hall, trailing his quilt. She straightened the rumpled bed once again, and he climbed in. He wanted to tell her that he had been crying because of a story in the *Times* about a big party on Staten Island, but the minute he got into bed he was overcome with sleepiness, and it seemed too complicated to explain. He would tell her in the morning, if he remembered. She turned out the lights, and Sperry went right to sleep.

Brush Twice Daily
and Go Easy
on the Bonbons

I was at my dentist's. I should have been relaxed, because it was only a cleaning and checkup, but I was suffering from a small, undeserved hangover, and the injustice of this made me edgy. I squirmed in the chair, trying to get comfortable, and closed my eyes against the bright nine-o'clock sun. My head pounded dully, and each scrape of the doctor's metal pick on my lower right molars reverberated unpleasantly in some deep interior echo chamber. My head was a cave, full of noisy spelunkers. I stirred, and the doctor's instrument pricked my gum.

"Hey!" I said. "Watch it."

"Oh-oh," said my dentist. " 'Fraid I made a booboo."

He squirted the gum, and I rinsed and spat. "God," I muttered under my breath. " 'Booboo.' 'Oh-oh.' "

The dentist glanced at me sharply through his rimless half-glasses and then turned and selected another pick. "Sorry," he said, scraping again, "but it's hard not to make a booboo when I'm getting off tartar."

For some reason, I was suddenly on guard. I tried to gauge the man, but the sun, bouncing off his spectacles, hid his eyes in an impenetrable dazzle. I decided to test him.

"How are my gums?" I said when he next straightened up. "Any signs of beriberi?"

"Just so-so," he replied, turning his back. "They'd be better if you'd massage them. I recommend two toothbrushes."

97

"Two toothbrushes!" I cried. "Here, here, you've gone too far."

"Sorry," he said pushing me gently back in the chair. "That was a bit rococo, I admit. A barbarity."

"Oh, I wouldn't say *that*," I said magnanimously.

"Yes, you would," he said, scraping on my uppers now, "if you thought about it."

I thought about it, and ground my half-cleaned teeth. Then I made myself lie back. I cogitated furiously, planning my attack. My headache was gone, and my mind raced ahead like some gigantic, avenging hound. The dentist was polishing now, but his concentration seemed uncertain, and I thought his hand trembled for a moment. It came to me that he was holding my jaw open in sheer self-defense.

Suddenly he turned off the humming brush. "Did you murmur?" he asked in a kindly voice.

"No!" I shouted. "I mean, uh, yes. I was only going to say that beriberi is less common among the Mau Maus than sleeping sickness, which is caused, of course, by tsetse flies."

"No doubt. Whereas Berbers sustain healthy gums on a day-to-day diet of pawpaws and couscous. Among the Shoshones—"

"Nothing else?" I said hastily. "No condiments? Not even chowchow?"

"Not even jujubes," he said. "Though they sometimes hunt the Persian songbird, or bulbul, which they bring down with dumdums and then bake into a savory pie, as delicious to them as is a baba au rhum to Coco Chanel."

"Yum-yum," I muttered faintly.

"Once, from a small put-put on Lake Titicaca—"

"Can't we leave these damn foreign countries you know so much about?" I snapped. "All those copies of *National Geographic* you get for your waiting room . . . It isn't *fair!*"

"Aye, aye, sir!" he replied at once, swinging the X-ray machine over my head. "Done and done! Let our causerie range, taking in the world *in toto*. What'll it be—show biz? Sports? Art, with its Neo-Dada trend? Or the more chichi world of the yé-yé set? We aren't old dodoes yet, are we?"

"Baseball!" I cried. "That pitcher, Bobo Newsom—"

"Was a lulu," he said heartily, inserting the X-ray film clamp between my teeth. "As were Jo-Jo Moore and Choochoo Coleman. And let us not overlook Kiki Cuyler. As Papa Hemingway once observed, Kiki was the Gogol of the—"

"Enough baseball!"

"Tut-tut, don't upset yourself. On to Broadway, then—the thespians. Why, only last week I saw Zizi Jeanmaire, Mimi Hines, Dede Allen, and Bibi Osterwald dining together at Zum Zum. Zizi sans tutu, natch. Lovely ladies! Admirable masticators! But no prettier, I must admit, than were Fifi Dorsay and Anna Sten, the go-go girls of an earlier camera era. I used to make goo-goo eyes at Fifi."

"But Anna Sten—" I began.

"Starred in *Nana*," he said softly. "Or were you thinking of the Sten gun, a pom-pom used in World War II?"

The X-ray clicked for the last time, and the dentist removed the plate and whisked the cloth from my neck. Only then did he notice my tears, my heaving shoulders.

"Come, come!" he said, patting my arm in a friendly way. "Cheer up. No cavities! There is nothing to fear."

My sobs grew louder. "Gub-Gub!" I wailed. "Gub-Gub. Dab-Dab."

"Pull yourself together, man," he said, peering anxiously at me. "I fear our little chin-chin has deranged you. You sound coo-coo."

"No," I whispered, snuffling. "I just remembered about Gub-Gub and Dab-Dab. Those animals in *Doctor Do-hoo-hoo* . . . In *Doctor Dolittle*. Gub-Gub the pig and Dab-Dab the duck. I used to love them so when I was a little bu-huh-huh . . . when I was a little boy. And then they went and put them into that awful m-movie with Rex Harrison. Oh, I wish they'd left my little animals alone!"

"To which I cry a hearty hear-hear!" said the doctor. "I much preferred the animals in *Lili* and the songs in *Gigi*." He dried my face with the cloth, straightened my tie, and then put his arm around my shoulders and helped me to my feet. While I attempted to collect myself, he rummaged in a box of lollipops and small toys he keeps for his younger patients and then pressed something into my hand. "Here," he said softly, "this is for you."

It was a Yo-Yo.

"Gee, thank you, Doctor," I said, delighted with my prize. "And I'll see you in six months."

He took me to the door and waved cheerily as I started down the hall. "Bye-bye," he said.

How They Brought the Bad News from Ghent (N.Y.) to Aix (Kans.)

(Note: A Full Transcript of This Nightmare, Recently Dreamed by a Source Close to the White House, Was Delivered in Advance to the Federal Communications Commission)

SCENE: *P. J. Contumely's, an unsavory, deplorably élite dive somewhere on the East Side of a totally unrepresentative large city on the East Coast, possibly Media, Pa. The lighting is crepuscular and unoptimistic, the ambience (by Ming Cho Lee) intellectual and confining, the décor French Provincial. A few un-elected network executives are hunched at the bar, occasionally adjusting their dominoes as they knock back absinthe Gibsons in anonymous silence. Three television sets are in operation over the bar, each tuned permanently to a different major network; each is bringing us the identical commercial at this moment—a scene depicting stomach acids eating away the moral fibre of a typical American family. In the darkest corner of the room, five men are discovered in whispered converse at a round table, which is illuminated by a single guttering candle. Somehow, they all look familiar to us, although each one reflects nothing beyond an urbane and assured presence that is seemingly well informed on every important matter. From their caustic, irrational chitchat, delivered in heavily inflected voices, we learn that they are hiding behind such unlikely pseudonyms as* HOWARD K. SMITH, ROGER MUDD, FRANK REYNOLDS, WALTER CRONKITE, *and* ERIC SEVAREID. *It is after five on a December afternoon, less than two hours before the Hour of the Wolf.*

SMITH (*lifting his glass*): Well, Roger, here's Mudd in your eye.

MUDD (*urbanely*): Har-har! Gosh, Howard, that's rich! (*They all chuckle appreciatively.*)

CRONKITE: Hey, where are the others? (*He looks at his watch.*) A hundred and two minutes to go and I'm absolutely dry tonight. I couldn't lift a thing from today's papers.

REYNOLDS: Same here. This holiday season is from Dragsville. All upbeat and . . . you know, *credible.*

CRONKITE: Yes. It's a good thing we can get together like this, *comme d'habitude,* and provide reinforcement for our shared parochial viewpoints.

THE OTHERS (*severally*): Right. . . . Yep. . . . Keerect. . . . Exactly what *I* was thinking.

SEVAREID: By the way, Howard, that was a lovely bit you had last night on the Pentagon's continuing silence about the cranberry-sauce scandal at Fort Riley last week. That blew my mind.

SMITH: Why, shucks, Eric, I sure do appreciate that. Coming from you. I mean, you handled the same news so beautifully yourself—I caught you on tape. The way you bore down on the fact that at least one of the culpable mess sergeants was a *Republican*—out of sight! And I really grooved on that quotation from Irma Rombauer.

REYNOLDS (*thunderstruck*): Irma Rombauer! I though we'd all agreed to throw in a quote by *Rimbaud!* Where's my head at? No wonder I got all those puzzled phone calls from the heartland.

CRONKITE: Oh, well, it could have happened to any of us, Frank. Unanimity's a hard taskmaster. I only wish we hadn't used up that story last night, though. I tell you, I'm worried.

MUDD: What about giving 'em some year-end musings? You know—a think piece, but with mood. I read something this morning that I liked. An editorial somewhere. Let's see. . . . I think it begins (*he quotes from memory*): "Now, as the lowering sun lies somnolent in nether circlet of the ancient solstices, and full winter taughtens the taproots of the humble back-yard dandelion in its frigid fist, the heart grows somber. It is still five weeks until Groundhog Day, eight before the first brave sugar maple (*Acer saccharum*) secretly—"

SMITH (*quoting with him in chorus*): "—opens its subterranean dendroid faucets. Only the gaily bedight chipmunk—"

THE OTHERS (*joining in*): "—and the brash, Boreus-defying chickadee (*Penthestes atricapillus*) remain to keep us morning company in this dark season—" (*They break off, laughing in surprise.*)

MUDD: Golly, we must have read the same editorial!

SEVAREID: Talk about coincidence!

SMITH: Now, I wonder where we all might have read that. (*He ponders.*) For the life of me, I can't remember. (*They all try to remember.*)

MUDD: I think it was some paper with a short name. Like *Trim* or *Tide*. Something like that.

CRONKITE: I've got it! The *Times! The New York Times.*

REYNOLDS: Right you are, Walter. Imagine all of us happening to see that one paper on the very same morning!

SMITH: Anyway, it's too cornball for us. I won't touch it.

SEVAREID: Me neither. It's *Kitsch.*

REYNOLDS: Pastiche.

MUDD: Actually, I *hated* it.

CRONKITE: Me, too.

(*Enter two men who look very much like* DAVID BRINKLEY *and* CHET HUNTLEY. *They are greeted effusively.*)

SEVAREID: Good evening, Chet. Good evening, David.

BRINKLEY: Ho, ho, ho! Cut it out, Eric.

REYNOLDS: What's the bad news, Chet?

HUNTLEY (*wiping his eyes*): You guys are too much!

SMITH: What'll it be, boys? Bourbon and branch water?

BRINKLEY: What a bunch of kidders. (*To the waiter*) The

usual, Giuseppe. (*The waiter returns, bringing glasses of Madeira.*)

CRONKITE: I don't want to spoil the fun, gang, but it's only ninety-eight minutes till air time. You want to handle the rundown tonight, Chet?

HUNTLEY (*taking a folder of news clippings and wire-service teletypes from his pocket*): O.K., but I tell you, it looks damn thin to me tonight, boys. Nothing here but sunshine. (*He riffles through his papers.*) Let's see . . . employment is up 1.3—2.9 in the Middle West. Seasonal hiring in the stores, mostly, but it's there. The biggest hominy crop in fifty years has been harvested in Mississippi. Cost of living down .02, coast to coast, thanks mostly to the White House switching to the less expensive spread for the hols. No riots, no tornadoes, no campus busts—vacation times there, too. Operation Intercept reported picking up thirty-seven bushels of pot in a Yippie-owned minibus, but it turned out to be Christmas wreaths for families of the Chicago police. A big, fat zero.

SMITH: It's hard to believe. Just no news at *all*.

MUDD (*grimly*): What about foreign news?

HUNTLEY: Zip. Wilson, Pompidou, Nasser, and Golda Meir are all skiing at Kitzbühel. President Thieu read "A Child's Christmas in Wales" aloud to Buddhist orphans. More troops are coming home. Bob Hope entertained the principals at the Paris peace talks. Willy Brandt is ice-skating on the Volga with the Russian General Staff. See what I mean?

CRONKITE: Any major speeches? Anywhere?

HUNTLEY: Last night? Only Governor Reagan, Eric Hoffer, Attorney General Mitchell, Roy Wilkins, Bud Wilkinson, and Billy Graham. And David Eisenhower talked to the National Barbers' Convention.

REYNOLDS: Cripes. A bunch of nobodies.

SMITH (*dispiritedly*): What did David talk about?

HUNTLEY (*riffling papers*): Uh . . . "Nape—Challenge to Our Times."

BRINKLEY (*brightening*): Napalm?

HUNTLEY: No. He means kids should keep their hair off their necks.

BRINKLEY: Ugh. Anything in sports?

HUNTLEY: Just those twenty-one upcoming bowl games, college and pro. And the President rolled a 134 on the White House bowling alleys last night, his highest score ever. (*A prolonged silence descends.*)

HUNTLEY: Oh, there is one little item here. Seems there's this weirdo commune out in Iowa, and last week some of the members happened to read the President's Christmas Proclamation. It really zapped them. The whole outfit reported themselves to the local Junior Chamber of Commerce and made a public recantation and confession of error. They cut their hair, bought new clothes, took out credit cards—the whole bit. Fourteen of them have applied for mid-term admission to the state aggie school. Several couples have gotten married and taken out ranch-house mortgages, and three former heads are buying a Pontiac distributorship. Some of the chicks are opening a school for baton twirlers, and nine ex-freaks have enlisted in the Marines. The kids are going to reënact the whole thing, along with a ceremonial burning of their love beads, on the Ed Sullivan show this Sunday. This is front-page stuff in the boondocks, of course.

MUDD (*gloomily*): It does almost sound like news.

CRONKITE: I just don't see how we can skip it. Unless it's a put-on.

BRINKLEY: No, Walter. Face it: it's arrant normalcy.

SMITH (*bitterly*): I just don't know what's happening to this country any more!

HUNTLEY: Wait, wait! We're off the hook, fellows. I just noticed. This all happened in *Des Moines*!

SMITH: So what?

REYNOLDS: Don't you see, Howard? We mentioned Des Moines only last month, when what's-his-name—oh, you know, the Vice-President—made some speech there. We can't go back to the same old dateline so soon. It wouldn't give a balanced, representative picture of these United States. I don't think we can risk giving the impression that *all* the news is being made in that little strip of land that lies between the Hudson and the Rio Grande. I don't know about the rest of you, but I won't touch it. Call it prejudice or narrowness, but I think your program has to reflect what your basic feelings are. I'll plead guilty to that.

SMITH (*tearing up his notes*): You're right, Frank, of course. I feel exactly the same way, now that you've made it clear to me.

CRONKITE (*relieved*): Whee-ew! That was a close one.

HUNTLEY: The trouble is, this still leaves us with nothing for tonight. (*Another gloomy silence. It is broken by* SEVAREID, *who clears his throat.*)

THE OTHERS (*hopefully*): Yes, Eric?

SEVAREID (*a patient, exhausted father*): Well, fellows, I don't know how to say this. Frankly, I'm disappointed. This is not the kind of hardened-newsman's attitude I expected of you. Back when I left Velva, North Dakota, and headed for the provincial East, I never believed I'd hear this kind dispirited Corn Belt belly-aching and—yes, I'll say it—this utter failure of cynicism, when we're only faced with a little bitty patch of good news. Now, shall we give up and settle for three evening news programs of nothing but Gelusil, or shall we knuckle down, pull up our socks, and just plain go to work?

HUNTLEY: We're with you, Eric!

SMITH: Lead on, chief!

SEVAREID: I knew I could count on you all. O.K., Frank, you hustle out to the phone and find what Averell Harriman's up to. Tell him the spot we're in. And say hello from me to Marie. (REYNOLDS *exits on the run.*) The rest of you, get out your pencils. First of all, who sets up the bowling pins when the President goes bowling?

MUDD: Why, it's one of those mechanical gismos. Over in the Executive Office Building—I rolled a couple of lines there only last week. You know, one of those machines that sweeps up the leftover pins and sets 'em down automatically.

SEVAREID: I thought so! And before that how were the pins set up?

SMITH (*puzzled*): By hand, I guess. The old way.

SEVAREID: Right. By that forgotten American, the pinsetter. And pinsetters in Washington must have been . . .

MUDD: I don't get it.

CRONKITE: Got it! They must have been blacks! So the President, in the act of encouraging physical fitness, has fired some faithful, septuagenarian, lifetime federal black employee—

MUDD (*scribbling furiously*):—thus abetting the omnipresent manufacturing interests while adding to the burden of technological unemployment—

BRINKLEY:—in our racially troubled capital! Zowie, what a twist! Wait until I get to Milt Galamison and Bobby Seale for quotes!

SEVAREID: Let's move along. About that bumper hominy crop. This morning, I got on the horn to Secretary Finch, just on a hunch, and asked him whether habitual ingestion of large portions of hominy might not have deleterious effects on the American stomach lining. He said he'd put the Food and Drug people right on it and then call me back.

HUNTLEY (*licking his lips*): And?

SEVAREID: And he called back and denied it.

CRONKITE: Whoopee!

MUDD (*puzzled*): I'm just a li'l ole Washington stringer, but I'm sure learning a lot tonight. If he denied it, why—

HUNTLEY: Show him, David.

SMITH: Do your thing, Dave.

BRINKLEY: (*blushing*): Oh dear. It's just this gift I have. It isn't *skill*. Oh, all right. (*He assumes a seven-o'clock tone.*) "Secretary of Health, Education, and Welfare Finch today denied that habitual ingestion of that favorite rural foodstuff, hominy, might be a cause of endemic gastrointestinal trouble in the Deep South belly." (*He pauses for two seconds and then slowly raises his left eyebrow.*)

SEVAREID: Beautiful, *cher confrère.*

HUNTLEY: There goes the hominy market!

MUDD (*holding down his right eyebrow with one hand*): I just can't get the hang of it.

SMITH: Now you, Walter.

CRONKITE: Well—if you insist. "Secretary of Health, Education, and Welfare Finch today hotly denied . . . buzz, buzz, buzz." (*He pauses for two seconds and then clears his throat.*) "Harrummpphh!"

SMITH: And hominy goes the way of old Tab and the passenger pigeon!

REYNOLDS (*entering excitedly*): Bingo, Eric! Averell Harriman is away for the New Year's holiday. He's—get this!—he's skiing at Sun Valley.

MUDD: I've got it, I've got it this time! Like, this weekend, while seventy million members of the silent majority lie back on their duffs drinking beer as they watch forty-eight consecutive hours of football on the boob tube, the eminent East Coast Democratic elder statesman and peacemaker—

SMITH:—a charter member of the effete Establishmentarian snobs—

MUDD:—returns to the American frontier to restore mind and spirit in lonely communion with mountain majesties—

HUNTLEY:—pitting the skill of his seventy-eight-year-old legs against icy defiles undreamed of in the fetid and housebound imagination of Mr. John Q. Vicarious.

(*They all burst into spontaneous applause.*)

SEVAREID (*rising*): Well, gentlemen, I think we're back in business. I'm proud of you all.

CRONKITE: Nothing to it.

BRINKLEY: As simple as A.B.C.

SMITH: Hee, hee, hee! David, you *kill* me.

(*Bound for their three studios, they exit together,* MUDD *still experimenting with his eyebrow and the others assuming their customary evening expressions of barely contained despair, as the curtain falls.*)

Send Now for
Birchbark Brochure

(A Nervous View of the Summer-Camp Wilderness,
Compiled Just after a Forty-two-Column Hike
Through the Back Pages of the *New York
Times Magazine*)

Camp Boot

The *only* summer camp operated under methods perfected by
the U.S. Marine Corps. Eight weeks of total regimentation
closely paralleling conditions at our "toughest" U.S.M.C. training camps. Manual of arms, close-order drill, character-building
fatigue duties; training in rifle, machine-gunnery, mortars,
bazookas, hand-to-hand combat, etc. Swamp bivouacs, beach
landings, village-burning, riot control. Season culminates in
six-day war games and attack under modern low-yield tactical
nuclear device. Entirely staffed by ex-"Leathernecks," under
command of a kindly, battle-hardened U.S.M.C. colonel (Ret.).
Boys 8-16. "You send us an adolescent, we send you back a
platoon commander." Box 34, San Diego, Calif.

Camp Eeyore

A Tiny Tots camp for play and dreams. 250-acre campgrounds
are an exact replica of setting in A. A. Milne's whimsical, beloved *Winnie-the-Pooh* books. Children live in Wol's House,
Rabbit's Lair, Piglet's "Trespassers W" retreat, etc. Daily "ex-

potions" to North Pole, digging of Heffalump traps, games
of Pooh-Sticks, picnics in Enchanted Forest. Boys and girls, ages
2-7. Joyful supervision by "Christopher Robin" and "Kanga"
(Mr. and Mrs. Hubert Joss). Write to Pooh's Place, Box 2A,
Lintel, Vt.

The Experiment in Substitute Civilization

What thoughtful parent has not wished to expose his over-
civilized teen-ager to the rigors of life in an untouched wilderness, jungle, or desert? What world-minded citizen has not
longed to open his privileged, modern home to a wide-eyed
child of nature? *Both* are now possible under the unique Teen-
Switch Plan devised by the Experiment in Substitute Civilization. Come June, you jet-dispatch your son or daughter to
Central Australia, Hokkaido, the Congo, or the Sahara, where
he will live with a carefully selected "typical" aboriginal family
under highly demanding local conditions; days later, you greet
an adolescent Bushman, Hairy Ainu, Pygmy, or Bedouin, who
will take up residence in the absentee's place! While your "lout"
forgets hot-rods and hard rock and masters tracking, skinning,
blowguns, native rituals, water discipline, a demanding new
language, and sheer survival, you have the joy of introducing
your guest to shoes, hygiene, eating with knife and fork, "Gun-
smoke," and Shea Stadium. A microcosmal stride toward
Utopia, open now to a few far-seeing pioneers. Highly recommended by psychiatrists, explorers, etc. Boys, girls: 13-18. Parents
must submit to tests for suitability, patience. Cost: about $15,000,
including visitor's passage, expenses, dental bills, etc. Box
008, Boise, Idaho.

Kamp Koan

The oldest and still the best Zen summer camp in the
Poconos. Let your child achieve *satori* in an unspoiled mountain
woods setting. Expert training in contemplation, forgetfulness,

brooding silence, loss of self, in the hands of an obdurate *roshi* (Zen Master). Swordsmanship, archery without targets, abdomen control. *Koan*-riddles and *haiku* under the stars; campfire tea ceremonies. Write for enigmatic rice-paper folder. Hiroshige Shimizu, Director; Box 287, New Rochelle, N.Y.

Spadesville

Are you (and we're laying it right on you) a Mister Charley? Do you sometimes wonder if your heavy bread and uptight ways haven't cut off your kids from the more vibrant, with-it life of the ghetto? Here's your chance to get straight and ease your ugly goddam conscience by exposing your own young ofay to the traumas of our new "Downward Bound" program. Six weeks of guaranteed separatism! Days and nights of unremitting hostility, street hustling, rats and roaches, welfare hassles, funky chicks, pig-baiting, etc., can mess up young minds for real—as you'll find out when (and if) li'l "Master Whitey" comes home. Counsellors provided (dig!) by special arrangement with the Detroit and Newark Police Academies. Write Muhammad Umbatta, Box 2-B, Roxbury, Mass.

Waggy Dell

Going to Europe? Planning an ocean voyage? Now you can avoid the pricks and arrows of guilt at the thought of your pet languishing in a stuffy urban kennel while you make merry abroad. Send Rover, Fifi, or Spot to the only "four-footed" resort in the cool Berkshires! Treat your pavement-tired dog to the joys of a summer on an old-fashioned New England farm. Supervised romps in the open country; cow chasing, cat treeing, rabbit digs; adventures with skunks and porcupines; swimming lessons. Special attention to overweight and cowardly dogs, terrier hypertension, etc. Raw meat daily. Entire program under supervision of A.K.C.-approved veterinarian. Dr. J. S. Schumpeter; R.F.D. 1, Upper Stringham, Mass.

Den-Ta-La-Ka

A special lakeside camp for young people with severe oral problems. Now your child's summer happiness need no longer be impacted by acute orthodontic embarrassment. Send your junior teen to Den-Ta-La-Ka for an eight-weeks' crash program in expert orthodontics in the relaxing company of the similarly afflicted. Daily treatments under the pines quickly dispel all fears of friendly counsellor-"Docs." Mastication and brushing "games" lead to a lifetime of sound dental hygiene. Membership in the camp's celebrated Fife & Bugle Corps fights malocclusion while encouraging music appreciation. Heavily fluoridated water from natural spring. Fresh corn on the cob. Entire staff graduates or students of accredited dental colleges. Send X-rays with application. Dr. Irving Karp, Box 2115, Bronx Station, N.Y.

Camp Wetback

"An adventure for budding social consciences." Let your junior sociologist learn by *first-hand* experience the frightful lot of migrant farm laborers. Campers "learn by doing"—long hours in the fields, harsh foremen, abysmal housing conditions, outdoor toilets, minimum pay. Ideally located on a 30,000-acre working sugar-beet farm in southern Colorado—not a model but the "real thing." Send for illustrated booklet. Mr. and Mrs. Reuben Horsfall, Alkali Flats, Colo.

Venus Dunes

At last, an opportunity to introduce your adolescent to the famed, much-misunderstood "natural" plan devised by the European psychologist Sandor Kovchak! In short weeks at this sun-blessed, coeducational seaside Illyria, youngsters learn to cast aside the inhibiting *pudeurs* of our guilt-haunted Calvinist civilization as they discover that "the answer to life is 'Yes!'"

Unsupervised, rules-free play, beside a sea as blue as that which lapped ancient Aegean shores. (Heterosexual "buddy system" protects swimmers.) Children come home beautifully tanned, with a new expression of detachment bred by affection, freedom, and trips. All games, sports "invented" by campers themselves. No expensive camp uniform, save sneakers and poncho. (Legal entanglements that abbreviated previous seasons recently solved by acquisition of sequestered 87-acre private estate in a mature community. No bail-bond guarantee now required.) Boys, girls: 14-18. Mrs. Hermione Collymore, Mr. Colin Walbridge; Box 4, East Hampton, L.I.

Life in These
Now United States

(The *Reader's Digest* Is Captured by the Enemy)

America Grooves

Officer Bob, who has directed traffic on our Main Street for as long as most of us can remember, saw a long-haired, typically "messy-looking" youth crossing against the lights one morning. He blew his whistle, stopping all traffic, and said, "Watch your step, Miss." When the teen-ager glared at him, the well-liked minion of the law smiled and said, "Oh, I beg your pardon. I thought you were a girl. You *look* like a girl."

"And you look like J. Edgar Hoover's grandmother in drag," shot back the youngster. He stepped closer to Officer Bob and said, "Listen, Fuzzhead, if you read anything besides *The Spanker's Monthly*, you'd know by now that hostility to unusual forms of male dress almost invariably conceals a repressed homosexuality, marked by hysteria and frequent episodes of enraged brutality. Likewise, if you could stop fondling the butt of the Smith & Wesson Police Special like some cornball Rod Steiger, you might notice that you've been wising off at the son of the First Selectman. My pop has his eye on you, *Sturmbannführer*, and you'd better, like, get on the stick."

The next morning, when the same young man appeared at Officer Bob's crossing, they had a briefer exchange. "Pig!" said the lad. "Punk!" muttered Officer Bob. That day, however, Officer Bob gave out forty-seven tickets for overtime parking, issued fourteen summonses to schoolchildren for loitering, and arrested an eighty-three-year-old grandmother for driving with a mud-spattered license plate. Now he is our town's Chief of Police. "I sure learned my lesson," says Officer Bob, twinkling. "The kids are where it's at." —Betty Birch (in the Iowa *Grunt*).

•

In addition to her duties as our school-bus driver and town clerk, my Great-Aunt Hannah, a widow, is a nudist. Every afternoon, rain or shine, she lies down on the glider on her front porch, as naked as a doorknob (see "Toward a More With-It Speech," p. 89.—*Ed.*), and reads *Sunshine and Health*, in plain view of all the traffic on Elm Street. As you can imagine, this has caused some "talk," but over the years our town has learned to put up with her little ways. "If we just ignore her," said the Rev. Gantry, the Jansenist minister, "maybe she'll knock it off. Or catch a bad cold," he added, chuckling.

Last fall, Aunt Hannah's granddaughter, Esther-Mae, went off to college at State U., and a few weeks later Esther-Mae's picture appeared on the front page of the new undergraduate paper there; she was taking part in a Grape Strike Pageant, and she was as naked as a darning egg. (Very good!—*Ed.*) Now Esther-Mae has moved to the East Village, in New York, where we hear she has embarked on a profitable film career, and lots of the kids in our town have taken to spending the afternoons with Great-Aunt Hannah on the porch, where they eat cookies and look at her picture books. As my husband says, "It only shows to go you—you can't knock tolerance!" —Alice Leonowens (from *The Pharmacist's Retort*).

Freaking Out Loud

I've discovered what's bugging my Dad—the F.B.I.!—Buddy Fliegelman, in the P.S. 92 *Grab-Bag*.

Marriage is a long sentence that begins with a proposition. —*The Christian Dentist*.

We had a prairie fire last summer, and by the time it was

over the whole town was smoking grass. Get it? —Tom Beeber (Petunia, Colo.).

I can read my Dad like a book—and he wears a plain brown wrapper.— Buddy Fliegelman, *op. cit.*

A Boy Named Ernesto

Another Boring Story from Everyday Life

One afternoon, many years ago, a rich American was having his shoes shined on a sidewalk in Cienfuegos, a city in Cuba. The ragged local boy on his knees before him was working away with a will, humming a native song and making the shoecloth pop. The American removed his Panama hat and wiped the perspiration from his brow with a silk handkerchief, and then puffed with satisfaction on his Havana cigar. It had been a good day for him. He was a broker for the United Fruit Company, and that morning he had concluded a profitable deal with a corrupt landowner that would halve the wages for several thousand local sugar-workers while simultaneously depriving them of their right ever to own bicycles. He had also arranged with the wily governor of the province to raise the tax on literacy—a plan that would swell the already bloated coffers of the infamous United Fruit monopoly. Yes indeedy, it was a good day!

The boy finished his labors, and the American handed him a counterfeit peso.

"No teep, señor?" asked the lad, with an impudent grin.

"No 'teep,' Pedro," said the man, tousling his hair. "Sorry 'bout that. The sooner you greaseballs learn to stand on your own feet and give an honest day's work for an honest day's pay, the sooner us gringos will be hotfooting it to Switzerland with the last contents of your Treasury. *Comprende?*"

"*Si, señor,*" piped the boy. "And *muchas gracias* for another valuable lesson in laissez-faire economics. I won't be needing your filthy lagniappe any more, for I'm off for the Sierra

Maestra." And he threw the lead coin in the man's face and strode away.

Only then did the American glance down and notice that the peasant lad had shined his nice white shoes with stove polish. He started after him with an oath, but the clever youngster had tied his shoelaces together, and the imperialist fell heavily to the pavement and fractured his pince-nez.

"*Ay, Chihuahua!*" cried the boy's mother, who had been watching this scene from the window of her slum. "Ernesto, come back! We will starve—and besides, you have forgotten to brush your teeth *con* Gleem!"

"I will be back, *Mamacita*, astride the wind of history!" cried the boy from the corner. "One day—I swear it to you, *madre mia*—this man's son will pin my likeness, in a giant poster, to the wall of his room at the Groton School!"

The ragged boy was right. Che Guevara was on his way!

Put-Ons: The Best Medicine

One evening last autumn, second graders at the Vapid Falls, Minnesota, elementary school locked their principal, Mr. Forbush, in a mop closet and proceeded to wreck his office. They burned the school records and stuffed Mallomars into his dictating machine. They poured ink all over his checkbook, mucilage in his rubbers, and raspberry Kool-Aid in his box of cigars. They tore down his picture of President Harding and played kickball with his globe.

The next morning, after the school janitor had released him from the mop closet, Forbush went directly to the second-grade room. "O.K., kids," he said to the class. "I'm ready to talk turkey. Amnesty for demonstrators is guaranteed. Compulsory naps are abolished. What are your demands?"

The boys and girls looked at each other in astonishment. "What demands, Mr. Forbush?" piped up Billy Fraser at last. "Gee whiz, haven't you ever heard of Trick or Treat?"

"Holy mackerel, I forgot about Halloween!" Forbush cried,

smacking himself on the forehead and laughing heartily. "The joke's on me, kids." Still chuckling, he expelled the entire class.

•

Hiram Warsaw, a nineteen-year-old Bronx dropout, grew tired of making obscene telephone calls one day. Instead, he looked up the name of the last man in the Manhattan telephone book and called him up. "Hello, Mr. Zzyzybyzynsky?" he said.

"Yes?" said Mr. Zzyzybyzynsky warily.

"I was just looking in the phone book and I noticed—"

"Yeah, I know, I *know!*" Mr. Zzyzybyzynsky shouted.

"Don't hang up!" Warsaw said. "Listen, I just saw you were the last name in the phone book and I thought I'd call you up, because my name is Aababonowicz and I'm the *first* man in the Manhattan book."

"No kidding?" said Zzyzybyzynsky, interested.

"Yeah, how *about* that!" Warsaw said. "I was thinking we ought to get together somewhere, Mr. Zzyzybyzynsky, and rap about our problems. I mean, we have a lot in common."

"Yeah, O.K., sure thing," said Mr. Zzyzybyzynsky eagerly. "Where shall we meet?"

"Oh, around the 'Ms' somewhere," said Warsaw, and hung up. The next day, in an inexplicable fit of ennui, he enlisted in the Marines for a four-year hitch.

New Hope for Lycanthropy

Thanks to the Treatment of a Courageous Backwoods Psychiatrist, Victims of America's Most Whispered-About Illness Are at Last Taking Their Places in Normal Society
[Condensed from *The Garageman's Almanac.*]

When Ralph Waldo Lupus, the only child of a wealthy Winnetka, Illinois, couple, was about six months old, his mother first noticed that he had long gray hair growing on his palms, but the family pediatrician assured her (wrongly) that this minor oddity would soon "clear itself up." Little Ralph Waldo's boyhood was happy and unnotable—with one exception. Approximately once a month, at the time of the full moon, he would have no appetite for his breakfast. Questioned by Mrs. Lupus, he invariably reported that he felt "full"—rather as if he had eaten several large hamburgers, cooked very rare, during the night. He also told about experiencing vivid dreams of running about the countryside "dressed up like a big doggy." His mother decided he had been reading too many comic books, and thereafter "cracked down" on his reading matter.

For some years, life went along smoothly enough for this typical American family. The only cloud on the Lupuses' horizon was the curious fact that they seemed unable to keep any dogs or other pets on their estate. A series of watchdogs—an Airedale, three dachshunds, a bull terrier, and a large German shepherd— vanished, one by one, after a week or two in residence, always apparently running away during the night. At the same time, Mr. Lupus noted the gradual dwindling of his herd of angora rabbits. One morning, after the hired man had reported the theft or flight of the family's prize Merino ram, young Ralph Waldo, now fourteen, slept very late and then breakfasted on four Alka-Seltzers. Mr. Lupus, pleading a sudden business engagement, packed a bag and hurriedly left the house, never to return.

Alone, and by now deeply concerned about her son's appearance, which seemed to alternate rapidly between emaciation and sleek good health, Mrs. Lupus began a six-year medical odyssey to find diagnosis and treatment for her boy. Across the land, diagnosticians, psychiatrists, dentists, and nutritionists examined Ralph Waldo, and, noting only an unusually rangy musculature of the lower body, pronounced him healthy and normal. At last, depleted in spirit and pocketbook, Mrs. Lupus brought her son last year to the rustic clinic of psychiatrist Dr. Jakob Pretorius, in northern Manitoba. Dr. Pretorius, a small, white-haired man with extremely thick glasses, examined Ralph Waldo for an hour and then sat down for a private chat with Mrs. Lupus.

"Madam," he said bluntly, "I know what you suspect."

"You do?" said Mrs. Lupus, blenching.

"You believe your son to be a victim of lycanthropy. In plain words, you think he is a werewolf."

Mrs. Lupus nodded, her face suffused with shame. "At last, it's out in the open," she murmured.

"Which is half the battle," said the good doctor. "Madam, I can help your son. I can even guarantee a cure. The fact is, Mrs. L., *there is no such thing as lycanthropy!* It exists only in the mind."

"But, Doctor—those howls in the night? Those scrabbling footstep on the porch roof?"

"Only the wind," said Dr. Pretorius.

"Those sudden changes in appearance?"

"Psychosomatic. You see, your son *believes* he is a werewolf, and so, secretly, do you. You are both victims of a delusion more common than is suspected. Why, *why* must we still go on whispering about lycanthropy! When will we rid ourselves once and for all of this burden of superstition and fear that has come down to us from the Dark Ages? Madam, this is the twentieth century!"

Dr. Pretorius sent Mrs. Lupus back to Winnetka on the next train, having explained that he would lock himself alone in a small room with Ralph Waldo on the night of the next full moon, which was to fall two days later, and then merely awaken the young man at the proper time for "a good, long talk."

A week later, Ralph Waldo Lupus came home, a changed man. There was a new confidence in his step, a ruddy flush of health in his cheeks. Indeed, he seemed so well, so mature, that Mrs. Lupus quickly agreed when he asserted that he wished to seek his fortune in Chicago.

Unfortunately, Mrs. Lupus was not able to thank Dr. Pretorius. His associates have told her that he disappeared on the very night of Ralph Waldo's cure, leaving only his shoes, notebook, and worry beads in the room. They believe him to be suffering from amnesia, brought on by overwork. It is sad he can't see Ralph Waldo Lupus today—a fine young man snatched back by intelligent psychotherapy from a social stigma that now, thanks to Dr. Jakob Pretorius, will be rooted from the darkest places of the American unconscious. Mrs. Lupus visited her son recently and noted with pride that he had gained fifteen pounds and two inches in the past six months. He is a rookie in the Chicago Police Department, assigned to park patrol, and expects promotion shortly.

•

Coming Next Month:
Black Power: The Miracle of the Electric Eel
Playin' My Axe: Harold Stassen's New Career as a Rock Musician
Let's Get in God's Bag
From Pot to Hash: Confessions of a Short-Order Cook
Human Encounter Groups: New Hope for the Post Office?
The Friendly Lepers of Katmandu
Getting Busted: The Truth About Those Silicone Treatments
And other articles of heartening credulousness!

The NCMSB Report

PREFACE TO THE 1970 EDITION

This fifth edition is, to put it frankly, useless. Ever since this famous 1965 article first trumpeted clear warning of the findings of the National Cultural Manifestations Sampling Board, each annual reprinting has been snapped up in universities and bookstores across the land, yet that gratifying response has never been followed by the faintest evidence that anyone *has changed his cultural patterns as a result. Today, we are not just slipping deeper into the cultural sink; we are down the drain. Every one of the dire predictions here has been precisely verified by events; the up-slashing curves made by extrapolations to 1970 in the original charts have proved in actuality to be even more sickeningly vertiginous. Even the mild hopes raised last year by the anti-cultural "good beginnings" of the Nixon Administration have been blasted. More recently, and only short weeks after President Nixon courageously invited Mr. Red Skelton to head the bill at a White House evening entertainment, the Chief Executive saw fit to journey to Philadelphia and there publicly and repeatedly clasp the hand of Leopold Stokowski! This example of unchecked cultural lasciviousness in the highest places suggests, to your editor at least, that there will not be a sixth edition of this document. Rome, it may be remembered, was also "cultured."* —Ed.

"Wake up, America! The hour grows late, and it's time, high time, each one of us faced up to his responsibility to *do* something about the culture explosion. The facts are here. The only question that remains is whether we have the courage to face them!"

These bold, frightening words form the epilogue to the long-awaited 1200-page report of the National Cultural Manifestations Samplings Board: *The Crisis of Responsibility in an Age of Cultural Excess.* The volume, a sobering bedside-table "must" for every American who has recklessly plunged ahead with his old concert-, art-gallery-, and theatre-going habits, who has bought and read poetry and criticism in thoughtless profusion, who has even invited comparative abstainers to share his profligate evenings at art-film houses, now confirms in bullet-hard detail what far too many of us have only dared whisper: *The culture boom is out of control!* No longer can we ignore or fail to understand the fact that mankind, especially in such overleisured areas as the eastern United States, is approaching the point of *total* cultural saturation at a dizzying rate of mathematical progression. At this writing, the number of Americans undergoing some cultural experience is increasing at the rate of 97.2 per minute; to put it another way, 22,860,119 citizens never previously exposed to culture have experienced an initial cultural contact* since the closing moments of President Johnson's Inaugural Address! This makes all too clear the stubborn persistence of our old posture of laissez-faire frontier optimism toward cultural overgrazing (*"Have you practiced your scales today, Sam?"*—Booth Tarkington), and warns of the appalling task that now lies in the hands of our arts demographers.

The NCMSB Report, compiled over a fifteen-year period by two hundred and seven sociologists operating under a grant from the Saturday Review Foundation, places a powerful new weapon in the hands of a few profoundly discouraged cultural Cassandras. Only last year, the long-hoped-for Cultural Wilderness Bill, which would merely set aside a few million virgin acres in Kansas and Oklahoma from hi-fi and theatre-of-the-absurd dep-

---

* Not including *The Sound of Music.* —*Ed.*

redation, was once again buried in congressional committee. Now, at least, solons will find it hard to dodge the sobering facts and statistics contained in the NCMSB Report's 426 tables and graphs. Consider, for instance, what lies immediately ahead for four of the East Coast's typical "culturally imploding" pockets. These sample areas—three square blocks in downtown New Hope, Pennsylvania; upper western Sullivan Street, in Manhattan; Madison Avenue from Sixty-eighth to Seventy-seventh Streets; and the South Shore of Long Island from East Hampton to Amagansett and inland to Springs—now contain an average of 522 culture-bound individuals per quarter acre, which is a gain of 297 per cent in four years. By 1970, their culture-practicers will have soared to a figure of 57 per square *foot*.* Culture "explosion"? Call it rather, a cataclysm.

Even when faced with these chilly figures, too many "free-culture" champions will probably fall back on their old shopworn clichés: "We can always spread out," or "There's plenty of room out West." But *is* there? Let them read page 872 of the Report: "In December of 1964, no less than 31 families in Sioux Falls, South Dakota, gave or received Jackson Pollock jigsaw puzzles for Christmas. In the Greater Houston area, 712 families now have Aubrey Beardsley matchbooks or Ernest Trova kaleidoscopes on their coffee tables; 49 per cent of those same coffee tables are in the culturally tolerable free-form 'Arp Shape.' " Clearly, the dangerous egalitarian cultural virus ("*I paint what I see.*"—Eisenhower) is raging unchecked from coast to coast.

Let us proceed to a consideration, necessarily brief, of the NCMSB's samplings and tables, concentrating on those pertaining to the critical Eastern "culture megalopolis." The mere titles of these statistical cross-slicings reveal the profound cogitation and systemic rectitude that so distinguish the work of the Report's authors. Here are samplings in three areas of cultural hyperactivity:

* A demographer recently attempting to check this figure in New Hope lost his ruler in the crush! —*Ed.*

1. *Vertical Culture*: "Weekend Hours Spent Waiting in Line Outside Guggenheim Museum; Outside Bergman/Chaplin/ Bogart Film Festivals; in Ticket Line at Y.M.H.A. Poetry Center (cumulative)."
2. *Visual Culture*: "Recognition of W. H. Auden/Susan Sontag/Thomas Schippers Among Passing Street Pedestrians" (frequency per week).
3. *Active Culture*: "Summer Weekend Hours Devoted to Active Culture: (A) In Western History to 1900; (B) Since 1950, Among Sample Either Playing Softball with Larry Rivers in Amagansett or Tennis with Elia Kazan in Fairfield County."

Classicists will notice at once the absence of such tried-and-true tests of cultural activity as "Hours spent reading," "Hours spent in museums," Hours spent practicing the recorder," etc. One of the NCMSB's most useful discoveries is the fact that these old standards are pathetically unreliable in statistical form, since they permit no evaluation of the depth of the culture subject's involvement in or understanding of his *Kulturwerk*. A man standing in front of Rembrandt's *The Anatomy Lesson* may be reminding himself to pick up some cold cuts at the delicatessen, and thus be at least momentarily culture-free; a man reading Burroughs' *Naked Lunch* may doze. By contrast, individuals in line outside a museum, or discussing or recognizing a cultural celebrity, are positively and inescapably *engagé*, in the Malrauxian sense. Consider, too, the startling unreliability of cultural *opinion* among samplees, as demonstrated in a puzzling and ultimately discarded NCMSB survey into audience understanding of Edward Albee's play *Tiny Alice*. Polled at regular intervals after the drama's initial appearance, playgoers at first divided almost equally, with 52.7% of those attending the previews claiming to understand the "meaning" of *Tiny Alice* and 47.3% admitting to confusion. By mid-December, 1964, the "Understand" group was strongly ascendant, claiming 80% of the total. A month later, however, there was a total rebalancing: 53.6% did *not* understand *Tiny Alice*, with the Understanders slipping down to 46.4%. By mid-February, 1965, only 11.1% still claimed to understand the play; non-understanding stood at a triumphant 88.9%. Extrapolating this curve, the experts predicted that total audience obscurity would be achieved a few minutes before noon on St. Patrick's Day of the same year.* Clearly, "meaning" in culture has become déclassé and statistically anarchic, and must be discarded.

On, then, to the three initial tables—so similar, so implacable in their deadly upward arrow thrust toward impending total cultural chaos.

To break in for a moment: the inclusion of Mr. Schippers, the conductor, in Chart 2 is a remarkable tribute to the perceptiveness of the sample-takers and the over-all reliability of these statistics. Originally, the third cultural celebrity in this test was Mr. Leonard Bernstein. Certain inconsistencies in the figures puzzled the experts, however, and investigation disclosed the prevalence of a remarkable degree of Bernstein-hallucination among the culturally overexposed. Otherwise reliable inter-viewees swore to having seen the celebrated conductor on Fifty-seventh Street, at the Central Park Zoo, etc., at times when he was, in fact, in Hollywood or in the Berkshires. Mr. Schippers was then substituted. The scrupulous NCMSB pollsters also devised a number of "trick" questions that served to weed out culture-dazed subjects who were, for example, unable to tell the difference between Miss Susan Sontag and such other major culture figures as Susan Stein, Gloria Steinem, Stephen Sond-heim, and Baby Jane Holzer. In the same fashion, they also eliminated celebrity-viewers who called the poet "Mr. Auden" or "W. H."—or, indeed, anything but "Wystan Auden."

---

* In point of fact, it happened at 4:55 in the afternoon of March 16th, 1965. Mr. Albee, on hand at a matinee to make note of the occasion, presented a ceremonial bouquet of forget-me-nots to Mrs. Hallie Starbird, of Tona-wanda, Md., who was the very last play-goer claiming to understand any part of *Tiny Alice*. Deeply touched, Mrs. Starbird thanked the playwright and then turned to a bystander and said, "Who was *that*?" —*Ed.*

CHART 1. WEEKEND HOURS SPENT WAITING IN LINE OUTSIDE GUGGEN-
HEIM MUSEUM; OUTSIDE BERGMAN/CHAPLIN/BOGART FILM FESTIVALS;
IN TICKET LINE AT Y.M.H.A. POETRY CENTER.

NOTE: In the appendix to the Report, the authors point out that
the foot of the weekend line outside the Guggenheim Museum has
recently come to within eighty-four feet of the foot of the line waiting
for the doors of the Metropolitan Museum to open, thus approaching
the conditions of absolute culture-mix that now prevail in the infamous
Third Avenue cinema ghettos.*

---

* How charmingly innocent, how childlike in its minuscule anxieties, this
warning looks today, in the darker light of our 1970 knowledge! It was
but two or three months after the initial publication of the NCMSB report
that the first overt incidents along the Guggenheim-Metropolitan border
were noted. Six weeks later, despite herculean efforts by neutralist media-
tors, the matter had exploded into the violent "Saturday War," which
saw the exposure of the infamous Fifth Avenue pretzel-sellers' counterspy
ring, the daring "Flying Nannies'" raid on the Guggenheim spiral, and
the reflexive ensuing capture and cultural disarming of two hundred
and sixty-three art lovers (including three trustees) from the very top steps
of the Met entranceway. The present state of truce in the mid-Eighties
blocks is, in the words of Hilton Kramer, "parlous," and the rival jostling
hordes of cultural zealots that still throng the disputed areas on weekends
and holidays, flaunting their catalogues and whispering aesthetic excoria-
tions, give scant promise of better times to come. —*Ed.*

CHART 2. RECOGNITION OF W. H. AUDEN/
SUSAN SONTAG/THOMAS SCHIPPERS AMONG
PASSING STREET PEDESTRIANS.

Note: (A) Miss Sontag as yet unborn;
Mr. Schippers an infant. (B) Mr.
Auden in Vienna; Mr. Schippers in
Spoleto.

CHART 3. SUMMER WEEKEND HOURS DEVOTED TO ACTIVE CULTURE.

CHART A: IN WESTERN HISTORY TO 1900.

CHART B: SINCE 1950, AMONG SAMPLE EITHER PLAYING SOFTBALL WITH LARRY RIVERS IN AMAGANSETT OR TENNIS WITH ELIA KAZAN IN FAIRFIELD COUNTY.

Note: (*X*) *Mr. Kazan indisposed for four weeks with tennis elbow.*

Now, what do these three tables tell us? At first glance, statistically innocent readers or irresponsible cultural zealots may be tempted to state that we are on the threshold of three "impossible" eventualities—that the Eastern culture group will shortly be spending all 55 weekend hours (5 P.M. Friday to midnight Sunday) standing in line outside culture meccas; that Miss Sontag and Messrs. Auden and Schippers will be recognized by everyone everywhere; and that Mr. Rivers and Mr. Kazan will have to spend *all* their summer daylight hours playing softball and tennis with culture companions. The answer: *exactly so!* To point out the obvious parallel, nuclear fission was also considered "impossible." We have arrived, in short, at our cultural Alamogordo.

Prolonged study of these tables allowed the Board scientists to theorize and then to confirm the existence among us of "cultural athletes"—individuals of almost unbelievable artistic stamina who were able, for example, to play tennis with Mr. Kazan on a Saturday morning, return to town and take their place in the queue outside a Chaplin Festival, and, while in line, recognize Miss Sontag, *en passant* across the street! From this was evolved the already famous Norman Cousins' Law: *"Culture is most practiced among the cultured."* This is possibly the most discouraging aspect of the entire crisis. It means that the very culture groups most in need of self-restraint and rigid culture-planning are most liable to cultural excess. These make up the shocking omnipresent hordes of the overcultured—the wan, hot-eyed families one sees alighting, with books, art catalogues, and guitars in hand, from their Volkswagens outside Lincoln Center and eagerly chattering as they hurry in to a fresh cultural experience that will "feed their habit."

The Board's ingenious development of the Mutchnick-Jamison Culture-Sensitivity Indicator permitted testing of some of this group against counter-samplings of a group on the cultural fringe and a group of cultural fellaheen (imported from Terre Haute, Indiana). The latter group had experienced no "Cult.-Stims." (reading the *Paris Review*, attending an Antonioni movie, buying a Bartók record, etc.) whatever; the middle group averaged less than one Cult.-Stim. weekly; the cultural élite (bitter misnomer!) was in need of at least five Cult.-Stims. weekly. The test measured physiological and emotional reactions to a typical Cult.-Stim.—the dropping of the name of Andy Warhol into conversation at 25-second intervals.

Chart 4 proves the *effects* of Cousins' Law. Note the total placidity and trustworthiness of Group A, the commoners. Note the beginnings, the faint warning twitches, of cultural excite-

CHART 4. NAME-DROP SENSITIVITY AMONG THREE CULTURE GROUPS.

ment among Group B that accompany each Warhol-drop. And observe, at last, the *increasing* agitation, shortness of breath, and nail-biting among the culture addicts at each repeated "Warhol." Can there be any doubt remaining as to the horrid nature of the crisis that is upon us?

What is to be done to halt the culture explosion? The picture is ominously clouded. Preliminary glowing reports of the efficacy of the oral anti-culture pill developed in a crash program of research at the Orrick Laboratories seem to have been overoptimistic; test subjects now report that their initial sharp interest in the stock market, golf, etc., seems to flag after three to four months of daily pills. Fresh chemical experimentation has been undertaken. Plain old-fashioned cultural abstinence, by contrast, is now frowned upon by most social scientists, since it runs headlong into the widespread "culture is good for you" mystique, and occasionally leads to such aberrant practices as reading *Life* in darkened rooms, attending the Trans-Lux East alone, etc., and a resultant heavy load of guilt. Selective choice of healthful cultural substitutes, once urged by the New School for Social Research, has also proved ineffectual, simply because "Cultural substitutes tend to become cultural" (Susskind's Hypothesis). Each attempt by small, pioneer culture groups to switch to a culture substitute—i.e., cheering the New York Mets, watching Busby Berkeley musicals on the "Late Show," playing whiffleball in Central Park—has led inexorably to a small cultural sub-explosion in that area, thus exacerbating the original problem.

At present, the only positive counter-measure appears to be disciplined adherence to the Cultural Rhythm System. Culture victims truly anxious to curb their old ways report considerable success as a result of daily temperature-taking and occasional weekend abstinence. They have learned to recognize the onset of the period of dangerous cultural hyperactivity, usually four to six days after the arrival of the *New York Review of Books* in one's mailbox. Temptation can often be avoided, especially on rainy weekends, by leaving town during this time, though trips to Westport, Tanglewood, etc., can lead to a "slip."

Realistically, however, it is asking too much of human nature to expect that such difficult voluntary sacrifices can bring the culture explosion to a halt. Next week, sixteen grim-faced top members of the NCMSB will pack bags, briefcases, and bulging cartons of blown-up data charts and take a train to Washington, where they have an appointment with congressional leaders.* Their message will be brief and fervent: The time has come for a federal program, backed up by the full power of the law, to put a stop to the culture explosion.

* Faugh! —*Ed.*

Fall Classic

(A Garland of Mixed Autumn Strophes Plucked after an
Evening of Aeschylus at the City Center, Followed Too
Quickly by an Afternoon of Mel Allen and the World Series)

SCENE: *A mighty concrete* theatron, *triple-decked, brave with
bunting and bright with October sunshine. As the action com-
mences, wealthy Athenians are still crowding the* diazoma *and
the* klimakes *as they search for their seats. In the center of the*
orchestra *we see the altar, a mound of earth topped with a
rectangular slab of rubber. On either side of the curving green*
proskenion, *there is a* paraskenion, *in foul territory, each containing a low shelter. From these shelters, from time to time,
appear heroes, arbiters, and godlings. Enter* MELALENDER, *a
soothsayer.*

MELALENDER:

Hail, all hail, fandom, and thrice welcome be
To our vasty temple, House That Ruth Built,
Parnassian shrine and *skene* once more
To our unconstrain'd autumnal revels,
Where this day, not unwitnessed, shall unfold
A fresh renewal of full sacred rites,
Capstone, you might wanna say, of another
Great season of the great Attic pastime!

Soon, before thy to-be-affrighted eyes,
Will appear right fell fiends, Reds from the house
Of the Cincinnati, boldly to wrest,
If wrest they can, the cup of victory

From the hands of the bestrip'd-flannel-clad
Atticans, children of Hephaestus' seed,
And holders—yea, again!—of the precious,
Hotly fought junior-circuit gonfalon!

Fiends, I said, though sworn am I by my vows
To dread Pallas to strict neutrality,
And therefore I adduce, most hastily,
Refutal: that, for all I wot, these bold,
Hot-eyed hordes from corn-belted Tartarus
May be good-conscienc'd, clean-limb'd fellows all,
Known for their reverence of hoary sires.
And now, pray, bend ears to this suasive plea.

CHORUS *(singing)*:

How are ya fixed for blades,
   Striplings and elders?
How are ya fixed for blades,
   Ye chin-tress'd elders?
(Murmured counter-refrain):
Hear the hymn we spout
O'er the victim sounding:
Deft, soft agoran shout
Sense and will confounding!
Round the soul entwining
Without lute or lyre—
Souls in madness pining,
   Wasting as with fire . . .
(Full chorus, drowning out murmurs):
'Cause a worn-out blade makes shaving mighty tough!

MELALENDER

(speaking from a perch atop the paraskenion, *as, below him,* HEROES *disport themselves in various classic attitudes)*:

Behold, the White-Haired One doth retrieve
   The back-smit pitch, and, mounded high,

Wins again the multitude's fealty,
    So mighty is the grasp whereby,
Heaven-holpen, he doth whirl and throw,
    Secondward, southpawwise, the ball,
Seized there in midflight by the eagle
    Kubek, who now, with feather'd ease,
Wafts the sphere to the initial sack,
    The taloned Skowron's lair, who feasts
Thereupon, ending the uprising!
    Wrathy Pinson and guileful Post,
Their mouths befouled with dust, both lie dead!
    This twin killing—hear, O ye fans!—
Eraseth a hallowed mark, long 'graved
    'Pon the tablet-screeds of the sport,
For One-to-Six-to-Three double plays
    Executed by the home team
In the third inning of the first game,
    In the modern Periclean
Era, and how, Attic fans, about that!

(*Scene shifts to an aperture in the* paraskenion, *within which,
in bored, easy postures, lounges an assemblage of* HEROES. *Enter
a bowlegged, lantern-jawed, horny-handed* GHOST, *clad in faded
flannels.*)

GHOST (*sepulchrally*):

Lo, what do I behold? My fellers all,
Mine erstwhile band of belaurelled heroes,
By o'erconfidence thus besapped again?
Do I roam scorned for naught? Awake and hear,
Ye fledglings of my brood! Look, look, alas,
Upon the shade of thy late Allfather,
So coldly bann'd by them that should have loved
The wise maunderings of his merry tongue.
Mark ye these wounds from which the heart's blood ran
When, not a year since, quite o'ercome we were

In the glutted haughtiness of our pride—
Felled by one mighty Mazeroskian
Four-ply swipe! Remember ye not that black day?
Awake, ye myrmidons! The footsore ghost
That once was Casey bids ye all arise!

HEROES (*severally*):

Cripes! . . .
        What do mine astonished orbs descry?
Is not . . .
        that ghastly spectre . . .
                the Old Man?

GHOST:

Know ye me not, my babes, my famed platoons?
Are ye too drows'd in pride to heed my pain?
Ho, Duren! Ditmar! Come forth from hiding,
And right eftsoons shall I put all to rights!

(*Enter* FURIES, *symbols of Front Office Ingratitude.*)

GHOST (*seeing* FURIES):

Nay, 'tis not to be. That this skipper's helm
Is not now mine had quite beslipp'd my mind.
A troop of shadows, legions yet unborn,
Strangely hight The Mets, haply shall battle
For the Ol' Perfessor, cross yon reeky stream.
Revenge me! To the Polo Grounds, to Thrace,
To Lemnos, even to the Three-I League
Must I fly, these baying hounds at my heels.

FURIES:

Follow, seek him—round and round
Scent and snuff and scan the ground!

GHOST *(sinking)*:

But who put my ketcher out in left field?

FURIES *(in a barbaric yawp)*:

Houk! Houk! Houk!

CHORUS *(gladsomely)*:

Grave priests of Acropolis,
  Youths in bosky glade,
Merchants in metropolis,
  Choose the Azure Blade!
    (murmuring again):
Round the soul entwining
  Runic words we wind,
Crumbling, cracking, mining
  The temple of the mind!
    (shrilly):
Oracles say, in their caves,
"Man, you never *had* such shaves!"

(There is a sudden grumble of thunder, and the CHORUS *exits hastily, casting nervous glances at the heavens. Enter* ORESTES *in the guise of a muscular blond right fielder. He falls to one knee and tensely executes some practice left-handed swings with a club.)*

ORESTES:

King Apollo, bright Hermes, Hercules,
And Hephaestian Foxx, look on me now!
A meagre boon humbly do I bespeak:
Send me this day but one fatted gopher
That I may thwack in Daedalian flight
Beyond the topmost rim of yon *skene*,
Heavenward ascending as sacrifice
To all thy ne'er-to-be-minished powers!

(Enter an eight-cylinder Chrysler Eccyclema, *a powder-blue job, with white-wall tires. It comes to a halt beside* ORESTES, *and from it steps the goddess* ATHENA, *who trips over her robe, then recovers herself.)*

ATHENA:

Far off I heard the clamor of thy cry,
Hummed on the wind instead of wings I came,
To charge thee, O not unseemly Earthling,
One full import-freighted question withal.

ORESTES *(grovelling)*:

Alack! I fear thy dreadful inquiry,
Great Queen. Methinks thou comest to punish me
For full many an impious blow struck
In o'ermuscled pride this half-twelvemonth past!
Dost thou come to thunder the heretofore
Murmured plaint of scribes—that in rank *hubris*
I have shaken the sixty-column'd shrine
Of the godling babe, the Sultan of Swat?

ATHENA:

Nay, arise, 'tis naught of that, sweet swinger,
Long since have you drear expiation done
In stare-ey'd nights unslept, in chances whiff'd,
In awesome pokes by stray zephyrs foul-blown.
'Tis but mine own small business brings me here,
One boon to beseech of *thee. (Simpering, she produces a tablet from her robes.)* Wouldst thou . . . uh . . .
Couldst thou, upon this tablet of purest
Wax, for Pallas, thy John Henry inscribe?

ORESTES *(obliging graciously)*:

Sure thing, Queen—here. Now hie thee off this sward
Before yon dark-garbed minions, in dogged
Duty, to thee the old heave-ho impart.

(He leads her away as she clutches the tablet happily to her breast. Enter CHORUS, *clearing its throat, but another growl of thunder causes it to change its mind. It withdraws in confusion.)*

MELALENDER *(from his perch)*:

Late it grows. Hespera's twin-hors'd chariot
    The Bronxian heavens hath quit.
Beclouded, shadow-smit, the blood-gouted tilt
    Unresolved before us sways!
Here, in ninth frame's nether half, the score, thick-tied,
    In Gordian gyves lies knotted.
Yet take heart, Atticans, for, lo, thy legions
    The enemy redoubts beclaw!
Whirlpits of despond whelm the Cincinnati!
    Loaded are the hassocks! One bingle
Shall waken shouts hereafter happy-thrilling,
    So don't go 'way, anybody!

SCENE: *A tense gathering of the Cincinnati at the central altar. Enter* BROSNAEUS, *a bespectacled philosopher and fireman.*

BROSNAEUS:

Hither, and not unsummoned by thy call,
O Skipper, I come, heeding thy wigwag.
There, unfar from where stand we atremble,
My four eyes espy the deep-browed Yogi.
His awful mace, unbloodied yet, doth cleave
The void air—aswish doth he cleave it now,
His Ajax-like practice riffles withal!
But enough. Hand me the pill and withdraw
Thy melancholy visage dugoutward.

(The Cincinnati disperse, leaving BROSNAEUS *brooding alone. He soliloquizes.)*

They swarm, they swarm, these bestripèd tigers!
The loathly blood is dripping from their eyes.
Welladay! In my deep-furrowed mind's eye—
Unmyopic orb!—the foredoomed outcome
Full plainly I see: but brief minutes hence
Curv'd goat's horns my double dome shall adorn.
Aloed irony that I, a poet,
With an E.R.A. of three point oh four—
A true servant of Euterpe, Clio,
And their seven sisters of Helicon—
Should fall, dust-strewn, spittl'd, and dishonored,
To such an hairy band of thewy-skull'd
Picture-book perusers! Out upon it!
Now shall I cry for righting of this wrong.
Great Zeus, hear me! Thy thrall is in a jam.
Descend now, in omnipotence baring
Thine arm; perforate these anthropophages,
And succor this oppress'd twirler-Sophist!

(*He pauses, looking upward, then shrugs.*)

Nobody home. These dactyls have wearied
Even the Allhearer. Cooked now am I.

(*He begins his warmup pitches.* CHORUS, *seeing its chance,
scrambles forward.*)

CHORUS (*chirpingly*):

How are ya fixed for σπάθαι,
    Peloponnesians?
How are ya fixed for σπάθαι,
    Shave without lesions!
Please make sure you have ἱκανάι,
'Cause a worn-out σπάθη makes shavin' mighty χαλεπόν!

(A colossal lightning bolt descends from above the Grand Concourse, accompanied by an infuriated roar of thunder. CHORUS *disappears in blue smoke. A cloudburst drops several billion gallons of wine-dark rain on the* orchestra, *scattering* HEROES, *arbiters, and Athenians, and quickly washing away the entire playing surface. Only* BROSNAEUS *and* MELALENDER *are left in view.)*

MELALENDER:

Wow! There it *is*, fans—five-o'clock lightning!

BROSNAEUS *(his face turned up in wonder)*:

This strain'd drama is now played out.
Somebody up there liketh me!

AFTERWORD TO *"Fall Classic"*

Time has so eroded this noble frieze that some archaeological footnotes must be appended. These warriors are engaged in the World Series of 1961, which was won by the Yankees over the Cincinnati Reds in five games. That was the season that Roger Maris hit sixty-one homers, breaking Babe Ruth's ancient record, and the year that Casey Stengel, after losing the previous World Series to Pittsburgh, was replaced by Ralph Houk as Yankee manager. Casey's Mets were as yet unborn, but the Furies did indeed follow him to the Polo Grounds—and beyond. In those tradition-ruled days, the Yankees were always in the World Series, and their broadcaster, Mel Allen, always handled the play-by-play, while Gillette paid for the singing commercials between innings—mellifluities that no longer echo in the porch

*of the national ear. Gone too are most of these heroes; of all
the baseball people here, only Vada Pinson is still playing.*

*The parody, inspired by a concurrent visit of the Greek Trag-
edy Theatre repertory company to New York, was written just before the World Series began, and it contains an accurate sporting
prediction—the "foredoomed outcome" envisaged by Brosnaeus.
He, of course, is Jim Brosnan, the Cincinnati relief pitcher and
author (his bullpen musings resulted in two good baseball books),
who got a terrible going-over by the Yankee hitters; unsaved by
the gods, he gave up nine hits, five runs, four walks, and two
wild pitches in six innings of work. The writer's lot is not a
happy one.*

Adeste Brentano's!

(A Premonitory List of This Year's Yuletide Offerings
in Coffee-Table Literature)

On the Wing!

Eleven years ago, Holger T. Whitby, president of the Amal-
gamated Brass Company of America, quietly began photograph-
ing houseflies with his family Brownie. Today, Mr. Whitby,
no longer a mere hobbyist, is recognized throughout the Nature
world as the photographic Audubon of insects in midair. Here
are over two hundred of his stunning full-page color portraits,
each in perfect focus, of midges, bluebottles, houseflies, ichneu-
mons, dung flies, mosquitoes, gnats, harlequin fruit flies, lady-
bugs, white-faced hornets, horseflies, seventeen-year locusts, etc.,
all caught in full flight. Many exciting head-on views. The text,
which was written by Mrs. Whitby during her husband's con-
valescence from a recent bout of malaria, includes many helpful
hints about lens settings, camouflage, and antihistamines that
will permit you to take up this rewarding scientific pursuit. $85.

The Tattoo Calendar

This handy, Phillips Brooks-style 1971 calendar is graced
with 52 full-page photographs of masterpieces by the world's
foremost tattooists. Week by week, you will be charmed and
fascinated by a fresh, startling design etched in human skin,
faithfully reproduced here in full color. Included are Maori
nose patterns, a classic "Mother" heart of the Scollay Square
Post-Impressionist school, Yokohama bicep flowers, and the
Duke of Middlesex's celebrated ventral panorama of the Isle

of Wight. The ideal gift for retired naval officers, dermatologists, etc. $7.50.

Christmas in the Senate

A joyous compendium of Yuletide sentiment from the hearts and tongues of America's most beloved senior solons. Includes eleven tributes to the Season of Good Will delivered in recent years on the floor of the Upper House just before Christmas adjournment, taken word for word from the pages of the *Congressional Record*. Some of the plums in this rich pudding are Senator Thurmond's memorable eulogium to the lowly mistletoe, Senator Hickenlooper's 1952 Christmas card to the Republican National Committee, and Senator Fong's touching "A Boy's Christmas in Honolulu." The volume also contains a 12-inch stereo recording of Senator Dirksen's annual reading of "A Visit from St. Nicholas" to the Senate pageboys. A gift that every American will be proud to find under his stocking. $18.50.

Seven Roads to Springfield

It has fallen to the Cambridge historian P. L. J. W. Hogwought to remind Americans of the costly legacy we inherited from the bloody, unappreciated campaigns of Shays' Rebellion. Students of Armageddon will find harsh, meaningful parallels to subsequent and more publicized wars in this meticulous account of the tedious winter of 1786–87. You will not quickly forget the ironic significance of General Washington's famous murmured aside, the overturned chairs during the angry Parcheesi match at Worcester Court House, or the curious and nearly fatal oversight by General Benjamin Lincoln's hostler. Seventeen pull-out war maps, 827 pages, plus a foreword by the Military Affairs Editor of the *Wall Street Journal*. $30.

The Fireside Book of Bowling

For the first time, the complete lore, literature, reportage, great art, and humor of the world's most popular indoor sport!

Vivid alleyside prose and poetry by Homer, Chaucer, Shake-speare, Pepys, Smollett, Jane Austen, Dickens, Dostoevski, Twain, Hemingway, Gide, Arthur Daley, et al., with kegling master-pieces of art by Veronese, Brueghel, Watteau, Renoir, Kandin-sky, and others. It's all here, from that long-ago Golden Apple rolled by Eris, through Sir Francis Drake's nervy game of bowls at Plymouth Harbor, right down to the celebrated Jersey-side strike scored by Madeleine (Babe) LaFonza in the twelfth frame of the 1968 Middle States Women's Finals at the Bethlehem Bolo-Mat Lanes! A ten-strike of a book, exactly right for the sportsman or sportswoman in your family! $17.50.

My Friend Dusty

One cold November evening, lighthouse-keeper Eben Gorsuch went to his closet to take out his old herringbone tweed jacket, only to find that the entire left lapel had been eaten away during the summer. Such was Gorsuch's larval introduction to Dusty, the lovable and remarkably intelligent clothes moth (*Tinea pellionella*), who became his inseparable companion during the eleven months they shared on High Saliva, the desolate beacon that stands guard over the dreaded Mumbles. Cap'n. Gorsuch's personal diary, already a runaway best-seller, recounts the joys, the tears, and the constant surprises of a relationship rare in the annals of lepidoptera or the sea. Now readers may share in those morning "wakeup games," the search for Dusty's secret mitten, the housekeeper's departure, and the accidental ·but epochal discovery of moth-ratiocination during a midnight game of solitaire. Most affecting is Gorsuch's ac-count of Dusty's last Michaelmas, a holiday that ended surpris-ingly when her master lit the candles for their festive *diner-à-deux*. In the words of Marlin Perkins, "This is an animal story not to be believed." Illustrated. $8.50.

Pablo Picasso's Golden Telephone Book

News last spring that all the telephone exchanges on the Riviera were about to be converted to digit dialling sent Gaby

Haze, owner of Madison Avenue's Valuta Gallery, scuttling to Vallauris to beg of her old friend Picasso the right to purchase his now useless bedside personal telephone memo book. After six weeks of bargaining, the protean modern master laughingly relented and released the priceless volume for the almost gratuitous sum of $82,000. Now, at last, you can share in this treasure, which reproduces, with absolute fidelity, all of Picasso's brilliantly offhand pencilled "doodles"—historic sketches that leaped straight from the genius's fecund unconscious while he was absorbed in conversation on *l'appareil*. Of particular interest is the massive, angry, and undeniably Cubist box that surrounds the enigmatic though typically tauromachian words *"Filets de bœuf—6 francs?"* Included, too (to the joy of art historians), are the former telephone numbers of the Picassos' wine merchant, baby-sitter, *blanchisseuse*, etc. The art event of the year! $50.

The Navajo Song Book

A treasure house of melody compiled after a dedicated ten-year study by three Bryn Mawr anthropologists and a drum-tuner from the Folk Art Division of the Library of Congress. Here are the stirring war chants, the water-toting grunts, the amusing canyon echo songs, the lively corn-shouts, and the endless dirge-like drought chorales that have made the Navajos the envy of neighboring, tone-deaf southwestern tribes. Now you and your family can gather around the piano and quickly learn such true American classics as *"Ta-Wa-Kipi Na-Pa Hiwa Pot-Awa"* ("I Have Lost Father's Rattle"), *"Wip-a-Po"* ("My Bride Is Worth Three Burros"), and *"Akiva-Klupa-A-Ah"* ("Sand in My Eyes Again-O!") All eighty-four songs carefully scored for piano, gourd, and war drum. Profusely illustrated with photographs of sacred Navajo song moccasins. $24.95.

Ainmosni

Insomnia is my baby. We have been going steady for a good twenty years now, and there is no hint that the dull baggage is ready to break off the affair. Three or four times a week, somewhere between three and six in the morning, this faulty thermostat inside my head clicks to "On," raising my eyelids with an almost audible clang and releasing a fetid blast of night thoughts. Sighing, I resume my long study of the bedroom ceiling and the uninteresting shape (a penguin? an overshoe?) that the street light, slanting through the window, casts on the closet door, while I review various tedious stratagems for recapturing sleep. If I am resolute, I will arise and robe myself, stumble out of the bedroom (my wife sleeps like a Series E government bond), turn on the living-room lights, and take down a volume from my little shelf of classical pharmacopoeia. George Eliot, James, and Montaigne are Nembutals, slow-acting but surefire. Thoreau, a dangerous Seconal-Demerol bomb, is reserved for emergencies; thirty minutes in the Walden beanfield sends me back to bed at a half run, fighting unconsciousness all the way down the hall. Too often, however, I stay in bed, under the delusion that sleep is only a minute or two away. This used to be the time for Night Games, which once worked for me. I would invent a No-Star baseball game, painstakingly selecting two nines made up of the least exciting ballplayers I could remember (mostly benchwarmers with the old Phillies and Senators) and playing them against each other in the deserted stadium of my mind. Three or four innings of walks, popups, foul balls, and messed-up double plays, with long pauses for rhubarbs and the introduction of relief pitchers, would bring on catalepsy. Other nights, I would begin a solo round of golf (I am a terrible golfer) on some recalled course. After a couple of pars and a brilliantly holed birdie putt, honesty required me to begin playing my real game, and a long search for my last golf ball, horribly hooked into the cattails to the left of the sixth green, would uncover, instead, a lovely Spalding Drowz-Rite. In time, however, some perverse sporting instinct began to infect me, and my Night Games became hopelessly interesting. As dawn brightened the bedroom, a pinch-hitter would bash a line drive that hit the pitcher's rubber and rebounded crazily into a pail of water in the enemy dugout, scoring three runs and retying the game, 17–17, in the twenty-first inning; my drive off the fourteenth tee, slicing toward a patch of tamaracks, would be seized in midair by an osprey and miraculously dropped on the green, where I would begin lining up my putt just as the alarm went off. I had to close up the ballpark and throw away my clubs; I was bushed.

It was a Scottish friend of mine, a pink-cheeked poet clearly accustomed to knocking off ten hours' sleep every night, who got me into real small-hours trouble. He observed me yawning over a lunchtime Martini one day and drew forth an account of my ridiculous affliction. "I can help you, old boy," he announced. "Try palindromes."

"Palindromes?" I repeated.

"You know—backward-forward writing," he went on. "Reads the same both ways. You remember the famous ones: 'Madam, I'm Adam.' 'Able was I ere I saw Elba.' 'A man, a plan, a canal: Panama.' The Elba one is supposed to be about Napoleon. Here—I'll write it for you. You see, 'Able' backward is 'Elba,' and—"

"I know, I know," I snapped. "But what's that got to do with not sleeping? Am I supposed to repeat them over and over, or what?"

"No, that's no good. You must make up your own. Nothing to it. Begin with two-way words, and soon you'll be up to sentences. I do it whenever I can't sleep—'sleep' is 'peels,' of course—and in ten minutes I pop right off again. Never fails. Just now, I'm working on a lovely one about Eliot, the poet. 'T. Eliot, top bard . . .' it begins, and it ends, 'drab pot toilet.' Needs a bit of work in the middle, but I'll get it one of these nights."

I was dubious, but that night, shortly after four, I began with the words. In a few minutes, I found "gulp plug" (something to do with bass fishing) and "live evil," and sailed off into the best sleep I had enjoyed in several weeks. The next night brought "straw warts" and "repaid diaper," and, in time, a long if faintly troubled snooze ("ezoons"). I was delighted. My palindromic skills improved rapidly, and soon I was no longer content with mere words. I failed to notice at first that, like all sedatives, this one had begun to weaken with protracted use; I was doubling and tripling the dose, and my intervals given over to two-way cogitation were stretching to an hour or more. One morning, after a mere twenty minutes of second shut-eye, I met my wife at the breakfast table and announced, "Editor rubs ward, draws burro tide."

"Terrific," she said unenthusiastically. "I don't get it. I mean, what does it *mean?*"

"Well, you see," I began, "there's this editor in Mexico who goes camping with his niece, and—"

"Listen," she said, "I think you should take a phenobarb tonight. You look terrible."

It was about six weeks later when, at five-fifteen one morning, I discovered the Japanese hiding in my pajamas. "Am a Jap," he said, bowing politely, and then added in a whisper, "Pajama." I slept no more. Two nights later, at precisely four-eleven, when "Repins pajama" suddenly yielded "Am a Jap sniper," I sprang out of bed, brewed myself a pot of strong coffee, and set to work with pencil and paper on what had begun to look like a war novel. A month later, trembling, hollow-eyed, and badly strung out on coffee and Dexamyl, I finished the epic. It turned out that the thing wasn't about a Japanese at all; it was a long telegram composed by a schizophrenic war veteran who had been wounded at Iwo Jima and was now incarcerated in some mental hospital. (This kind of surprise keeps happening when you are writing palindromes, a literary form in which the story line is controlled by the words rather than the author.) Experts have since told me that my barely intelligible pushmi-pullyu may be the longest palindrome in the English language:

MARGE, LET DAM DOGS IN. AM ON SATIRE:
VOW I AM CAIN. AM ON SPOT, AM A JAP
SNIPER. RED, RAW MURDER ON G.I.! IGNORE
DRUM. (WARDER REPINS PAJAMA TOPS.)
NO MANIAC, MA! IWO VERITAS: NO MAN IS
GOD.   —MAD TELEGRAM

My recovery was a protracted one, requiring a lengthy vacation at the seashore, daily exercise, warm milk on retiring, and eventually a visit to the family psychiatrist. The head-candler listened to my story ("Rot-cod . . ." I began), then wrote out a prescription for a mild sedative (I murmured, "slip pils") and swore me to total palindromic abstinence. He told me to avoid Tums, Serutan, and men named Otto. "Only right thinking can save you," he said severely. "Or rather, *left-to-right* thinking."

I tried, I really tried. For more than a year, I followed the doctor's plan faithfully, instantly dropping my gaze whenever I began to see "POTS" and "KLAW" on traffic signs facing me across the street, and plugging away at my sleepy-time books when I was reafflicted with the Big Eye. I had begun to think that mine might be a total cure when, just two weeks ago, nodding over *Walden* again, I came upon this sentence: "We are conscious of an animal in us, which awakens in proportion as our higher nature slumbers. It is reptile and sensual, and perhaps cannot be wholly expelled. . . ."

"Ah-ha!" I muttered, struck by the remarkable pertinence of this thought to my own nocturnal condition. Thoreau himself had said it; I could never quite escape. To prove the point, I repeated my exclamation, saying it backward this time.

I did not entirely give way to my reptile. Remembering my near-fatal bout with the telegram, I vowed to limit myself entirely to revising and amplifying existing palindromes—those famous chestnuts recited to me by my Scottish friend. The very next night, during a 4 A.M. rainstorm, I put my mind to "A man, a plan, a canal: Panama." Replacing de Lesseps with a female M.I.T. graduate, I achieved "A *woman*, a plan, a canal: Panamowa," which was clearly inadequate; she sounded more like a ballerina. Within a few minutes, however, a dog trotted out of the underbrush of my mind—it was a Pekinese—and suddenly redesigned the entire isthmus project: "A dog, a plan, a canal: pagoda." I went to sleep.

Napoleon led me into deeper waters. Bedwise by night light, I envisioned him as a fellow-sufferer, a veteran palindromist who must have been transfixed with joy to find the island of his first exile so brilliantly responsive to his little perversion. But what if the allies had marooned him on a *different* island in 1814? Various possibilities suggested themselves: "A dum reb was I ere I saw Bermuda," "No lava was I ere I saw Avalon," "Lana C. LaDaug was I ere I saw Guadalcanal." None would do; the Emperor's aides, overhearing him, would conclude that the old boy had fallen victim to aphasia. A night or two later, I replaced Boney on Elba and retinued him with a useful and highly diversified staff of officers and loyal friends—a Rumanian, a female camp follower, a Levantine, and a German. These accompanied the Emperor by turns during his habitual evening walks along the cliffs, each feigning awe and delight as the impromptu musing of the day fell from his lips. "Uncomfortable was I ere I saw Elba, Trofmocnu," he confessed to the first. To the female, smiling roguishly and chucking her under the chin, he murmured, "Amiable was I ere I saw Elba, Ima." The next evening, made gloomy by the rabbinical sidekick, he changed to "Vegetable was I ere I saw Elba, Tegev." He cheered up with the burly Prussian, declaiming, "Remarkable was I ere I saw Elba, Kramer!" but, finding the same man on duty the following night (the list had run out, and new duty rosters were up), he reversed himself, whining, *"Un*remarkable was I ere I saw Elba, Kramer, *nu?"*

That seemed to exhaust Elba (and me), and during the wee hours of last week I moved along inevitably to "Madam, I'm Adam." For some reason, this jingle began to infuriate me. (My new night journeys had made me irritable and suspicious; my wife seemed to be looking at me with the same anxious expression she had worn when I was fighting the Jap sniper, and one day I caught her trying to sneak a telephone call to the psychiatrist.) Adam's salutation struck me as being both rude and uninformative. At first, I attempted to make the speaker more civilized, but he resisted me: "Good day, Madam, I'm Adam Yaddoog," "Howdy, Madam, I'm Adam Y. Dwoh," *"Bonjour,* Madam, I'm Adam Roujnob." No dice. Who *was* this surly fellow? I determined to ferret out his last name, but the first famous Adam I thought of could only speak after clearing his throat (*"Htims,* Madam, I'm Adam Smith"), and the second after falling down a flight of stairs (*"Yksnilomray!* . . . Madam, I'm Adam Yarmolinsky"). Then, at exactly six-seventeen yesterday morning, I cracked the case. I was so excited that I woke up my wife. She stared at me, blurry and incredulous, as I stalked about the bedroom describing the recent visit of a well-known congressman to Wales. He had gone there, I explained, on a fact-finding trip to study mining conditions in the ancient Welsh collieries, perhaps as necessary background to the mine-safety bills now pending in Washington. Being a highly professional politician, he boned up on the local language during the transatlantic plane trip. The next morning, briefcase and homburg in hand, he tapped on the door of a miner's cottage in Ebbw Vale, and when it was opened by a lady looking very much like Sara Allgood in "How Green Was My Valley," he smiled charmingly, bowed, and said, *"Llewopnotyalc,* Madam, I'm Adam Clayton Powell."

When I got home last night, I found a note from my wife saying that she had gone to stay with her mother for a while. Aware at last of my nearness to the brink, I called the psychiatrist, but his answering service told me that he was away on a month's vacation. I dined forlornly on hot milk and Librium and was asleep before ten . . . and awake before three. Alone in bed, trembling lightly, I restudied the penguin (or overshoe) on the wall, while my mind, still unleashed, sniffed over the old ashpiles of canals, islands, and Adams. Nothing there. Nothing, that is, until seven-twelve this morning, when the beast unearthed, just under the Panama Canal, the small but glittering prize, "Suez . . . Zeus!" I sat bolt upright, clapping by brow, and uttered a great roar of delight and despair. Here, I could see, was a beginning even more promising than the Jap sniper. Released simultaneously into the boiling politics of the Middle East and the endless affairs of Olympus, I stood, perhaps, at the doorway of the greatest palindromic adventure of all time— one that I almost surely would not survive. "No!" I whimpered, burying my throbbing head beneath the pillows. "No, no!" Half smothered in linen and sleeplessness, I heard my sirens reply. "On!" they called. "On, on!"